cordee

# MOUNTAIN BIKING
# TRICKS AND TECHNIQUES

## MARTYN ASHTON'S
## GUIDE TO BIKE RIDING SKILLS

Mountain Biking Tricks and Techniques © 2010

Published by Cordee, 11 Jacknell Road,
Hinckley, Leicestershire, LE10 3BS, UK
www.cordee.co.uk

ISBN 9781904207641

Design by Farrelly Atkinson Ltd (www.f-at.co.uk)

Printed by PrinterTrento Srl, Italy

Photography by Robin Kitchin (robinkitchin.com)

**Photographed riders:** Chris Smith, Lance McDermott,
Steve Peat, Danny MacAskill, Rowan Johns (World's greatest
Postman: Thanks for website video edit and design),
MartynAshton, Alex Trimnell, Grant 'Chopper' Fielding,
Blake Samson, Sam Pilgrim, Rachel Atherton, Gee Atherton,
Dan Atherton, Hans 'No Way' Rey, Oli Beckingsale, Steve Geal,
Jim Davage. Danny Holroyd, Vincent Hermance,
ey, Petr Kraus, Ricky Crompton
llery at www.mtbtricks.com

# CONTENTS

Foreword                                        5

Introduction                                    6

**Ground rules**                                8

Safety equipment                               10
Flat pedals                                    11
Location                                       12
Know yourself and your limits                  14

**Getting started**                            16

Limitations of your bike                       18
Bike set-up                                    24
Equipment                                      26

**Gaining confidence**                         30

Left from right                                33
Front foot                                     34
Urban furniture                                35
Grass banks                                    36
The 8-Track                                    36

**Starting to impress**                        38

Balance                                        40
Lifting the front wheel                        44
Lifting the rear wheel                         48
Bunny hop                                      52
Riding down steps                              58

**Adventurous riding**                         64

Track stand                                    66
Skid control & power slide                     70
Wheelie                                        76
Side bunny hop                                 82
Wheelie drop off                               88

**Getting Rad**                                94

Take-off & landing                             96
Style – start moving that bike around         100
The Scrub: or just keeping it low             106
Transition ramp drop-in                       112
X-up                                          120
Taking your limbs off                         124

**Trials Demon**                              130

Going Up (wall, log or step)                  132
Control Movement 1 Front-hops                 136
Control Movement 2 Endo                        142
Back hops                                      148
Trials drop-off & back-wheel control          154
Rock walk and Rock walk drop                  162
Side Hops: up and down                        168

**Freeriding genius**                         174

Manual                                        176
Fakie                                         182
Free-riding rolling drop-offs                 190
The Wall ride                                 194

**Dream tricks**                              200

Progression                                   202
Begin to spin: the 360                        204
Get upside down: The Backflip                 210

**Great places to ride or chat**             216

Mountain bike centres                         218
Skate parks                                   220
The community                                 222

"I just take each race one at a time and enjoy every single minute of it, and still do today! The only way to improve is to love what you're doing."

**Steve Peat**
World Cup Champion and
2009 World Champion

# FOREWORD

**A**s a tiny kid I was always chasing my older brothers around our local Park on bikes. They rode fast and pushed me to improve - I learnt a lot from them. They helped me learn how to tackle big jumps and the basic racing skills that serve me today but they also taught me the fun stuff like skids and wheelies; things that really made me love bike riding. I know this 'fun riding' was instrumental in the rest of my career - I'd learnt great riding skills but also had bike riding in my heart. Martyn's tuition in this book feels so familiar because it's based on that enjoyment of riding the bike, not just the technical aspects of getting fit or winning races, that stuff will take care of itself.

I met Martyn a long time ago, when I was just 19-years of age. Back then I'd just started racing Mountain bikes, mainly Cross country because Downhill hadn't got going yet, I progressed straight into the DH scene as soon as that kicked off. A few race wins got me noticed by the magazines and it was on photo-shoot trips that I got to know Martyn better. I remember seeing him riding for the first time, it was clear he had awesome ability matched with a clever way of breaking the components of a move down so he could attempt them. That 'Trials rider' mentality served him well. He'd watch us trying something and then go think about it for a while, return and nail it!

Like myself, Martyn can handle many styles of riding so we always have great fun pushing each other. I remember one time in Spain when things got pretty sketchy! Martyn had spent days driving around, scoping the land for cool things to ride, eventually finding this dangerous gap between two buildings (it was about five floors up!)

I was up for trying it and there was no way Martyn would stand by and watch me take the glory. We attacked the gap with very different styles, me more speed and downhill aggression; Martyn more trials and smooth finesse. The pictures turned out great and the shoot made the front cover of Mountain Biking UK. It just goes to show you can approach obstacles in different ways but the fundamentals are the same. Martyn will show you the fundamentals and keep you smiling all the way. I am so happy that Martyn decided to write this book. One of the true 'nice-guys' of the sport who rides for the right reasons... Enjoyment!

Cheers,

**Steve Peat**
*2009 World Champion*

# INTRO DUCTION

**I** started riding bikes professionally 17 years ago, I've been learning ever since and one thing I learnt over everything else, there is always more to learn, you can always improve. I've noticed that because I've tried many styles of riding from traditional Mountain Biking to BMX, Road riding to Dirt Jumps. I've even dabbled in a bit of tandem riding and unicycle over the years! I've discovered that 'the bike rider' is the same individual no matter what bike he/she is on. Sure there are differences in fashions and style, but the enthusiasm and passion for their bike is always the same.

So I'm teaching skills on various mountain bikes in this book but the basics are useful to any rider, and the progression later could work for a BMX rider just as well as it could for an MTB rider. The cross-over between disciplines is so vast now that the MTB is just a generic bicycle to me – I'm a bike rider – that simple and I'm happy to be your friend no matter what bike you ride (I'd like a go actually – what is it?)

I've made sure this book will apply to you whether you are an experienced rider or literally just starting out. The format is based on inspiration rather than step by step tuition. You will find that the trick 'recipes' get less and less based on technique as the book progresses. This is because at the beginning you should be thinking about traditional basics that will teach a strong riding position and

foundation for progression. As you develop, the visual elements I use should become more and more informative as you begin to understand how you and the bike interact.

The words will be the starting point of inspiration; the pictures show technical points but also the finished article in all its glory. Then use the website podcasts to demonstrate the move so you can then get out on the bike and start working on the move with reason and confidence. The mantras of each move are all you need take out with you, they should remind you of what you've read and seen – you shouldn't be riding around and looking at the book – muscle memory and visualisation is what you need to focus on. Then it's just down to enjoyable practice and watching the learning curve steepen every after every trick.

So thank you for picking this book up, thank you for the interest in bikes, I promise you will never regret learning a bit more about what you (and bike) are capable of. Right from the start have an open mind and never let yourself think "I can't do that." You can and most probably will.

Go online and visit www.mtbtricks.co.uk for videos and tutorials

# GROUND RULES

I am going to be talking throughout this book about the fun and enjoyment of riding bikes. Learning any one of the skills in this book will have a hugely rewarding sensation to it, along the path to mastering any of these moves you will likely be smiling. However from the very outset I want to be absolutely clear about the risks and likelihood of accidents that can occur when riding bikes. I am not just talking about the inherent dangers of pushing your personal riding limits; rather the absolute ordinary dangers of stepping over a bike and taking a totally normal ride. That simple pursuit of enjoyment

is dangerous; it is dangerous no matter how good you are on your bike. I have mastered many bike riding skills and witnessed true genius by professional friends of mine, but to this point I have never come across a rider that is immune to being hit by a car travelling at 40 mph. Similarly I have never been able to find anyone who has a head, arm, knee or any body part for that matter that was unaffected by hitting the ground at faster than walking pace. I don't wish to put you off at the very beginning but for us to progress it is essential we get off on the right foot - or should I say pedal

# SAFETY EQUIPMENT

These are most obvious requirements, the helmet being by far the most important. You can purchase a suitable helmet from many stores but I would always recommend you try and buy from an experienced cycle retail store rather than a supermarket or toy store. An experienced cycle store will be able to steer you towards the current technological advancements and make sure you are looking at helmets that fit you correctly, and are suitable for your requirements. I would recommend something along the lines of a modern open face 'free-ride' mountain bike style helmet to begin with, they have every aspect covered; light weight, comfort fit, peak, venting and rear head cover. Any helmet is better than none but spending a bit of cash protecting your noggin is something I would strongly suggest. A simple rule to remember from here onwards, if you are riding your bike, you must wear a helmet.

Your choice of protection after the essential helmet is up to you, it really depends on what you feel comfortable with, some riders are comfortable with gloves, and some are not. The very same stores that sell the helmet will stock an array of padding for your body, limbs and hands; some are for 'Extreme' jump riding some are for Down-Hill racing, try stuff on and see what feels comfortable. At points through this book I will note where I feel padding is necessary, and there will be points later that I will strongly suggest that it is time to purchase some good knee or elbow pads, hopefully by that time you will be very glad to spend a little more on your skills. For now I would rather focus on a basic set up that will allow you to move freely and in an environment that will be forgiving should you have a tumble.

# FLAT PEDALS

It is important to begin learning using a flat pedal. Flats as they are known will ensure that you learn correctly and can get free of the bike when things go pear shaped. To accompany the flat pedals, look to be wearing a comfortable pair of riding shoes, something like a traditional skate board shoe is perfect. Any sport training shoe will do but a flat sole is going to grip to the pins or teeth of a flat pedal much better. Experienced riders note; if you have become accustomed to clip pedals then now is the time to replace them with flats. All the moves in this book need to be learnt on a flat pedal so you have the correct control, once learnt properly all moves can be transferred back to clip pedals.

# RIDING
# LOCATION

Where we practise is very important, to begin with it needs to be somewhere that allows cycles. The perfect terrain to attempt all the moves in the first half of this book is on turf. A playing field, garden or down the local park, as long as bikes are allowed, will be the perfect area for learning the basics, the forgiving grass will mean you can make mistakes without serious consequence. Try to ensure that your chosen training ground has some public footfall, I went riding up in the local hills once and had a big crash, fortunately nobody was around to witness my mighty mistake, and the isolated area meant nobody saw, phew - pride intact! Unfortunately that also meant I sat up there with a broken ankle in the cold for quite a while before anyone noticed I was missing and thought about looking for me. A mobile phone in your pocket will also help with these kinds of problems and also comes in very handy when you get an annoying puncture and can't ride home. Your bike also happens to be a great place to sit and chat with your mates; riding with someone else also helps avoid the safety issues described above. However riding with friends is more than just a safety tip; you will have much more fun and learn quicker if you do it with someone else of similar ability. The camaraderie and helpful direction makes the learning easier, it is also very comforting seeing someone else struggle just as much as you. This is also a time to recognise that bike riding is something that can be done by all the family. The current statistics for healthy lifestyles are alarming, so getting out on a family bike ride once a week can only be a good thing. If this book helps inspire you to try that and discover how great riding with your family can be then it will have been worth all the hard work. Bike riding is

for everyone, and should be seen as an ecological form of transport, an amazing hobby and an exciting adventure vehicle that young and old can and should enjoy.

Later in the book we start to become specific with the obstacles and places you need to find to learn some of the advanced moves. At this time I will point you in the right direction to sourcing these places (such as skate parks and foam pits) so there is no need to worry about learning to back flip your bike in the garden for now, all the moves, no matter how difficult they seem now are on a learning curve. When you reach them none will seem as daunting as they do at the beginning.

Go online and visit www.mtbtricks.co.uk for videos and tutorials

# KNOW YOURSELF AND YOUR LIMITS

Again the beginning of this book is about basics and simple moves. If you learn everything in the first half of this book then you will be a very good bike rider indeed. Learning the entire book will see you riding at an exceptional level. It is more likely that once you have the basic moves mastered then you'll likely start to pick and choose your way through the book. That's perfectly fine; all of the tricks stand alone and can be approached from a fresh direction. As you progress it will become clear what suits your style and what doesn't. Go with what works and enjoy your riding; moves that elude you to begin with will probably pop into place at a later date anyway. Even learning the basics will see you move way beyond that of the average rider. All the moves from that point on will still have content and tips that apply to your everyday riding. The stories, fabulous pictures and podcasts will be great fuel to inspire you out on a day when inspiration has failed you. We all have limits and getting to know them is part of the

process; it's the same with your bike, you need to know about your bike's capabilities, I'm getting ahead of myself, don't worry about the bike just yet, we will get to that in Chapter Two.

Patience is going to be very important. I cannot stress this enough; you have to learn at a pace that suits you and you only. One day you may master two important elements and feel great. On other days it may seem impossible and you will struggle over a move for weeks. Try very hard to focus on the enjoyment of learning and the process that it involves. Even when you're trying something over and over, even when that trick just won't work, you are still learning. If you keep your patience and control you will get there in the end. If you find yourself really stuck then try something else, go back to the things you have learnt and enjoy doing them. As the confidence returns so will your interest in the moves that have evaded you thus far.

Lastly I want to congratulate you on your

progress; that's right, well done. You may only feel like you have read a single chapter of a book, big deal. Well actually you have come along way already, simply by reading through that short chapter we have made sure you are safe, thought about a place to ride and possibly who with. Also we have established that it isn't all roses, you may find some of this stuff really challenging.

You also learnt that even if you only learn one single element on the following pages then your riding will be vastly improved; learn half the book and you will be an exceptional bike rider. After the basics you are in control and can start to find out what type of bike rider you really are. One thing I guarantee, it will be a far better bike rider than you think.

"There were only 50 guys on the start line who had all worked for this for years and someone was going to ride away with an Olympic Gold round their necks. It still makes my hairs stand up when I think about it."

**Oli Beckingsale**
UK National Cross
Country Champion

# GETTING STARTED

**I**f you have a bike that is similar to anything mentioned in the following chapter, you'll be able to get going straight away. As your skills improve so will your decision of whether you need to upgrade your bike or not because later in the book you will find the moves and techniques are asking more of you, and your bike. To happily handle all the fun this book can throw at it, a bike just needs some working brakes and a quality frame. I'll mention again: your local dealer will be more than happy to let you know what your bike is suitable for, chatting with you local bike shop is also another important stage in becoming a better rider. They will know all the local rides that are fun, they will also know about local skate parks and fun spots you could go and become part of the local riding community. So try and get to know the shop and its workers – they are invaluable help in progressing.

# LIMITATIONS
# OF YOUR BIKE

It will go without saying that your bike needs to be of a suitable design to attempt the skills in this book. The modern mountain bike (MTB) is a great bike to learn these moves on, and even the very cheapest version is suitable for learning the basic moves in this book. However there are so many disciplines of cycling these days that there are numerous styles of bike that you could use. Here is a brief guide to what's what and how it relates to the skills you can learn here.

# TRADITIONAL MOUNTAIN BIKE

There is no such thing as a standard mountain bike, the sport has so many disciplines that the bike has developed in those areas to suit. What most people would recognise as a 'standard' MTB is this: 26-inch wheeled bike with lots of gears, with 'knobbly' off road tyres and front suspension forks. The frame will be of strong design and the more you spend the lighter the bike will be – using materials like aluminium and carbon fibre in the more expensive models. If this description loosely fits your bike then you have the ideal bike to start learning these skills.

# MTB - CROSS COUNTRY FREERIDE

These bikes include front and rear suspension and plenty of gears – some as many as 27 – and have 26-inch wheels – as do all MTBs. They have become the most popular mountain bike today and they really are very useful bits of kit. The technology advancements mean that £500 will get you a very useful bike indeed but you can spend well over £3000 on them if you like. There are 'cheap' bikes that include front and rear suspension but steer clear if I were you – suspension that will work and last doesn't come on a bike cheap bike. Trust in your local bike dealer for advice here, and with all other bike purchase queries – they will make sure that you get what you need – don't buy bikes from places that also sell groceries – always use a bike shop.

# BMX

BMX stands for Bicycle Moto Cross and first became popular in the early eighties, remember ET? The early BMX events were all about racing, and that discipline still has strong activity, it's even in the Olympics. However the BMX bike that would work for learning moves in this book would come under the title of 'freestyle'. A freestyle BMX is built to be very strong and can take huge landings from jumps in skate parks and dirt jumps, and just like the race bikes from which it's evolved, it has 20-inch wheels. The street scene is also very strong in BMX and some bikes are designed specifically for this urban form of riding. One limitation to a BMX, at least where this book is concerned, is that you don't have the option of changing gears. A capable rider could still get by using just the one gear but it will be more difficult to learn some of the moves.

# DIRT JUMP
# MTB

This is the 26-inch wheeled version of a BMX – single speed like a BMX but usually incorporates some front suspension that you wouldn't find on the 20-inch wheeled BMX. The Dirt Jump MTB is a very sturdy and tough bike that will handle all manner of bumps and knocks – again you have the downside that it's just one gear but if getting some 'air time' floats your boat then this will be a serious consideration later in the book.

# TRIALS BIKE

The Trials bike is designed for riding over obstacles and is almost always 'rigid' which means it does not have suspension. Along with being 'rigid' the Trials bike shares another similarity with a BMX, it also has just one gear. That is where the similarity ends though.

A Trials bike has very low gearing – meaning it is very easy to pedal – but can't go very fast. The geometry of a Trials bike is also quite unique; very long wheel base

and a very low seat height – so the rider can move around as much as possible.

Trials bikes aren't as common as traditional mountain bikes or BMX but you will see them quite a lot in this book - because I'm a trials rider. The techniques of trials riding are based in balance and control so will be very useful for you, no matter what bike you have. *You do not need a Trials bike for any moves in this book.*

23

# BIKE SET-UP

For nearly every move in this book it is important to set the bike up in the following manner when learning. Some of the moves are intended for cross country trail riding, and things like a low seat and flat pedals are unlikely but in the learning stage it is just way easier to learn with a simple set up that will make the learning curve all the more steep.

Make sure your bike is set-up using the following guidelines.

**Seat Height:** Run your seat as low as possible when learning the tricks. It is easy to get caught up on your seat and you need to get used to moving around on your bike for control. A quick release seat clamp could be a great early purchase so you can adjust this at any time, that's what I do on my bike.

**Brake levers:** Adjust your levers so they are in easy reach. I like having them slightly higher than usual but start with them at 45degrees. Ride with the levers in this position for at least one ride then adjust to suit if it doesn't feel comfortable. If you do adjust them keep the change small, you will really notice the difference.

**Tyre pressure:** don't get too stressed about this, just run your tyres at the recommended pressure on the tyre walls. They will be slightly harder than you need for ideal grip but at this stage you need to avoid punctures, they are a pain and slow down the process of having fun on your bike. As you get more serious and adventurous your friendly bike dealer will be able to advise on tyre choices for what you are planning.

**Gearing:** There is no right or wrong gear to be in when riding your bike, only the gear that suits you at the time. Don't be afraid to change the gears about, modern systems can put up with a lot of abuse. As a general rule when practising the basics, ride in a versatile gear that is easy to pedal but still has enough grunt to get some speed. Really the gears are there to experiment with and it won't be long at all before you find the gear that suits you. As a very rough guide: if you are attempting slow speed moves then ride in the smallest ring on the front rings (crank-set) and a large sprocket on the rear wheel – this will make the bike easy to pedal. For faster moves, move up to the middle ring (if you have three) or top (if only two) at the crank-set and into a medium sprocket at the rear wheel – this will give you a bit more 'grunt' to get some speed up.

If you have a single speed bike then don't panic, just ride it as it is. Only the slow speed moves will prove slightly more difficult but certainly still do-able.

# GOOD IDEAS

Here are some important items that you should think about taking along on your adventures.

**Multi Tool:** this is a suggestion for something you should look into purchasing, especially at this early stage when seat adjustment and lever position will change as you get used to the bike. They come in many different shapes and sizes, they are also of different quality but by no means do you have to use an expensive one. The tool I have in my cross country back pack cost an unbelievable £1.99 at the local bike store. If you are carrying a puncture repair kit or spare tube then think about a tool that has tyre lever devices for removing the tyre.

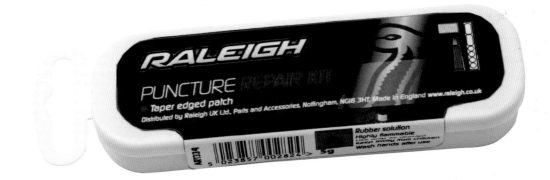

**Puncture kit/Spare tube:** on a long ride I would strongly recommend carrying a spare inner tube or a puncture repair kit. Your local bike shop will have plenty of products that you can choose from for help in a flat tyre emergency. If you have never changed a tube or fixed one then ask your dealer about it, it's really easy and he will be only to happy to provide some helpful tips on how to go about it.

**Pump:** Essential if you want to be able to repair punctures or fit a spare tube. The choice of mini pumps available is astounding and they could be the difference between a long walk home, or a quick repair.

**Stick these in your pocket:** Mobile Phone, chocolate bar and a quid: I will be honest, as much as I think you should carry all of the spares I've mentioned so you can fix a nagging problem like a flat tyre, the stuff that I always have with me is my mobile phone and £1 in my pocket. As previously mentioned the mobile is an emergency device, I just don't go out without it. The real piece of mind comes from the quid though. Sometimes mobiles don't have service, a pound can help make that call to your loved ones when the bike has broken and you need a lift. The quid can also buy you that emergency chocolate bar when fuel has got desperately low. The magic pound can also secure a bus ride home when something has snapped, I've done this on several occasions.

Go online and visit www.mtbtricks.co.uk for videos and tutorials

**Nutrition:** This is as simple as sticking a Mars Bar (other chocolate bars are available) in your pocket. So often we go out on our bikes with the aim of being back for lunch, things go well and all of a sudden you have been out way too long. The bar in your pocket can make a ride home a far more enjoyable trip once you have fuelled yourself. I love having some chocolate in my rucksack on rides, it is something to look forward to after a couple of decent climbs, a little reward for all the hard work I'm putting in. Obviously there are other well known chocolate bars available and all will do just as good a job. If you want some really useful sport nutrition bars then check them out at your local bike dealer – he will have plenty to choose from with all the info on why one is more suitable for you than another. If you aren't too bothered then just stick with the old Mars bar.

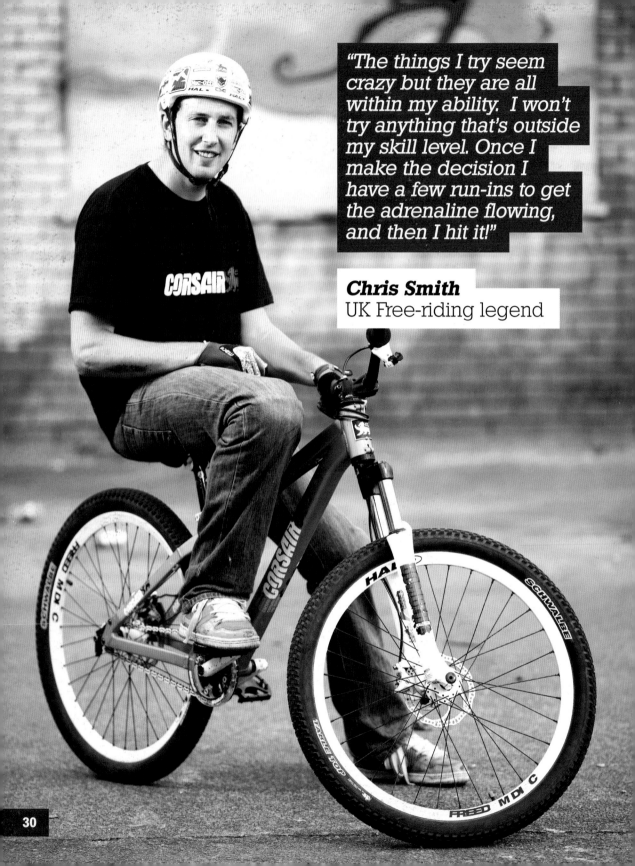

"The things I try seem crazy but they are all within my ability. I won't try anything that's outside my skill level. Once I make the decision I have a few run-ins to get the adrenaline flowing, and then I hit it!"

**Chris Smith**
UK Free-riding legend

# GAINING CONFI-DENCE

**B**ecoming a decent bike rider is all about gaining confidence and finding your limitations. Often when you test your ability it will be immediately evident that you're a lot more capable than your first thoughts. It's also healthy to realise in a small number of cases that you do have limits and this is the time to judge what your riding capability is. No matter what you think about your riding at this point - rest assured that the confidence in ability will grow as you work your way through the book. I know that to be true because that is the whole secret to improving your skills; it's simply trusting your confidence and taking control of the

OK we are all set up and ready to ride, the fun can begin. What we want to establish from the outset is a comfortable and confident riding position. That is going to be borne out of you mastering balance on your bike. This does sound like it could be difficult and perhaps a little boring. A moment of contemplation and calm at this is stage is going to create a few rules that will make everything else in the book make sense.

We aren't going to literally practise your balance whilst rolling along, you will be doing that all the time without knowing it. What I want you to learn is what I call the 'approach position'. This rolling position will be how you approach every obstacle or move from here on in, so it is quite important.

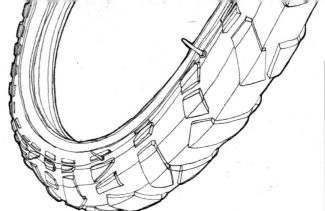

# LEFT FROM RIGHT

This is going to sound obvious to anyone who has ridden a bit, but many riders have overlooked this simple process, and although they've learnt left from right, they haven't done it in a way that is instinctive, causing a moment's doubt on the approach to a corner or obstacle, not good. So stand over your bike, feet on the floor at this stage bike, and pull the left hand brake leaver. Which brake did it operate? Some people will say "your left lever is the rear brake, stupid!" well not necessarily because in mainland Europe the brakes are flip flopped with the front on the left, rear on the right. We aren't interested in how the different countries run their brakes, or how your mate does it, all we are interested in is your bike, the bike you are going to learn on. So pull that left lever and by rocking the bike back and forth you should be able to determine which brake is operating. Once you are happy with what brake the left hand lever is operating (as I said, in the UK it's most likely the rear) do the same with the right

lever. The lever operating the front brake should give you a different response to the rear brake when it is held on and the bike rocked back and forth between your legs. The front will have a more definite response, and if you hold it you will discover that it is possible to lift the rear wheel easily by pushing forward. Holding the rear brake and rocking the bike back and forth will feel slightly vague as the bike will not move backward, but will drag forward. To get the operating systems embedded take the bike for a gentle roll around and spend a bit of time slowing and stopping, using just the rear brake. Really try to drum it in that this is the rear brake. The same again using only the front brake, begin gently with this lever as it will have a very drastic response if jammed on, you could get pitched over the bars.

This process should get you used to which lever does what, and also realising that each brake creates a different effect to the bike, this will be important later on.

Go online and visit

for videos and tutorials

# FRONT FOOT

Now you are happy with the braking controls we need to establish a very important technique that I can assure you will make you a better rider almost immediately, and over time will ensure you approach obstacles, tricks, corners and jumps with a relaxed and confident style - your approach position. I'm writing this book with my right hand, I simply couldn't do it with my left. The same applies to my riding; I ride with my right foot forward. It is very important that you learn which is your front foot. Now you are thinking about it, the answer may be obvious, if not try standing with both feet together and having a friend give you a gentle shove from behind. You should clearly have one foot that instinctively leads as you try to regain balance. Do it several times and it will become clearer. What ever foot it is, that is the pedal you should lead with, by that I mean this; when you are rolling along not pedalling, you should always have your pedals level with your lead pedal at the front.

# URBAN FURNITURE

Hopefully the ride down to your local park is adaptable for this, I find it a very useful way of warming up and also finding urban versions of things I will find out on the trail. I use all the local scenery as a way to get in the move and experiment with my bike. I love getting into that play-ride feeling, skipping along really light on the pedals, enjoying the heightened sense of acceleration things like alleys and subways provide. Big obstacles like steps and walls should be approached with caution but if you start at a level that is easy enough you will soon gain confidence and be bashing down some awesome urban descents in no time.

The important thing to remember on these in-between rides is that you're out playing, don't feel silly, and don't hold back, just enjoy yourself and the bike. Ride the stuff that is fun for your level, don't kill yourself or anyone else. This is another area where a riding partner can be awesome; racing around on a little urban route can feel great.

Curb stones and steps are all over the place and can be a way of bumping your way into a controlled style.

We will cover riding steps later in the book but don't overlook the tiny riding gem outside your house. Curb stones may look small and boring but they can be a wonder of play riding that will reap huge benefits. The key here is again imagination, don't see a curb, see a thirty foot drop-off, or see a series of slalom turns that will get your turning ability into tip top form. I play on curb stones more than I'd like to admit; in fact I consider it an important tool, even now, in my training as a professional rider. The beauty of this obstacle is they're everywhere and the skills and confidence that can develop from this awesome little obstacle are invaluable.

To start with use the breaks in each stone as slalom posts, dropping down one stone then turn to ride up, missing one stone and up the next, miss a stone before you again drop down the next. This can be done really slowly to begin, and then speeded up once the confidence has grown. If you struggle in the beginning then simply miss two stones between turns. If you are thinking that is beyond you then let me tell you that I have been in a car park with some of the finest riders in the world, all of us playing at this, trying to go faster or smoother then each other. It just never gets boring and once you are going up and down consecutive stones then it's like the moment in Rocky when he catches the chicken "Now you got speed!"

# GRASS BANKS

Get to know how your bike reacts under strain. On your local ride use your imagination to identify some banks to play on. The perfect bank is around no matter where you live it's just waiting for you to find it.

Once you have spotted a bank start to look at it in different ways. It isn't just a hill to go up or down. This is a multitude of turns, ascents and descent scenarios for you to play with. If you have a couple of banks close to each other, then you are really in business. Create a turn on the bank and then hit it in different directions, this will again get you used to the weight balance of the bike in turns, try and notice how the bike un-weights as you come up the bank with pace, this will keep you aware of how different angles change the way your bike react, especially if you have suspension. When you are on the trail this will be really important once you know what to expect from your bike it is only a matter of time before you start looking forward to those sensations and seeking them out. This eagerness for sensation is what you are looking for, through this it will become so much easier to learn, because you will be hunting the skills rather than waiting for them to happen, a big difference.

# THE 8 TRACK

I came up with this idea when teaching a friend to get some confidence on a local route he was riding regularly; he was an experienced rider but hadn't realised he was approaching left hand corners with uncertainty. Feeling unsure when turning is fine, having a weak turning direction is fine, knowing you have it and finding a way to set up is the important thing. This little 8-track will get you all clever about your strengths and weaknesses on cornering, braking, acceleration and pedal set up.

When you buy any video game, there is always a section of the game that is set aside at the beginning as the place you go to safely learn techniques. You need to identify a similar spot, a grass area that has some undulation to it, maybe the local park? This spot should have public foot fall, so help is never far away. Once you have that spot in mind venture down there and start riding (sitting down, gear versatile) in a figure of eight on flat grass, if you want use two trees to help create the track, if you're lucky the trees might bring some undulation to the ground and make things tricky. After about ten laps of your 8 track it will be start to be visible and easy to follow. So now stand and pedal between the criss-cross of the track, and roll the corners with your front foot forward. Keep this up so you find a rhythm for the pedalling, always ending so your front foot is forward by the time you reach the corner. You should have also created enough speed whilst pedalling to coast the whole corner and then pedal it to speed to achieve the same at the

opposite end. This process will establish a confident approach to corners and get you recognising some order in the pedalling and position.

If you are out with a friend then maybe have a game of cat and mouse on the little loop. Start at opposite apexes of the track and see who can catch who. This is awesome fun and will get you thinking about how to increase speed. After riding the track for a while try dropping your outside pedal down whilst in the corner, you will find that it more natural to lean the bike by doing this, so greater speed and grip will be possible. Make sure you get back onto the front foot for acceleration though.

I've had hours of fun with this 8-track, it doesn't matter how good you get, this will always find your limit. Practice will really pay off and you are bound to feel the benefits on the next corner you attack.

"I crossed the line and I just new I was World Champion! All my training and practice had paid off – I was on top of the world – literally!"

**Gee Atherton** UCI World champion - downhill

# STARTING TO IMPRESS

**T**his is the part where you leave the average rider behind because nearly everybody who rides bikes will find the following moves very difficult without having looked at them closely and understood what is going on. Once you've nailed a few of these opening moves then your riding will have moved forwards in leaps and bounds – you will literally have transformed as a bike rider.

# BALANCE: REALISE HOW GOOD YOU ARE

**H**owever before we get stuck into the art of balance, let's establish an important rule for the rest of this book. I want you to approach each trick whether it's these simple balance practice skills or a back-flip, with exactly the same riding position. As you go into a move, your body position will change for that specific trick. The approach position I am focusing on here is the stance I want you to adopt as you commit to the process I'm teaching you in each move. So, as you approach these balance orientated moves - and then every move from here on in - ride at it like this.

**Approach stance:**

- Stand on level pedals
- 'Front foot' forward
- Arms and knees slightly flexed
- Two fingers covering the brakes (takes practice but you'll get used to it)

**OK, so we have a clear approach to all the moves in this book. Let's get down to riding bikes and improving those skills. After this first balance practice I promise you will feel way more confident at riding your bike than when you first opened this book. This can be practised on curbs or the spacing lines in car parks, or even whilst riding down the road, use the double yellow line down a quiet street (safely please).**

Let's look at it on a curb because I love them. The aim is to get as far along it as possible, simple right. Well, try these little tips to get a record distance. Keep your eyes fixed on a distance in front of about two metres, don't stare at the front wheel, you won't last long. Keep your knees flexed and approach the curb with speed to roll, front foot forward - your approach position. Move the bike in between your knees trying to keep your shoulders central over the curb, head in line with the curb, looking about 2 metres along the curb ahead of you; don't look off the edge or that's where you will end up! This is another important rule to make habit at an early stage; always look where you intend to go, not what you are avoiding. Practice is what will make you a better rider, with balance it is about learning to relax, letting your body move. I used to have a metal pole in front of my house when I was young. I'd spend hours walking along it, trying to perfect my balance for riding. The pole was about two feet off the ground and it went for miles up the road we lived on. I remember getting about a mile along it on a number of occasions. It got me so centred with balance that it has never left me, I can even tight-rope walk now. You don't need this geeky level of balance though, so stick with balance practice on the bike, way more fun and

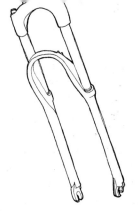

# " ALWAYS LOOK WHERE YOU INTEND TO GO, NOT WHAT YOU ARE AVOIDING "

you will soon be hunting out things to ride along that would have seemed impossible before. I find that setting goals or challenges is a great incentive; it helps me to see I'm improving. So use the cracks between curb stones to mark how far you can get. Start by trying to ride along without touching the tarmac or riding off the drop and onto the road for as long as possible, if you can do three curb stones in a row, award yourself with a smile/pat on back/chocolate bar – a roast dinner when you have made it to twenty stones in length. Although don't be too generous with your reward; I'm hoping this is a journey of constant achievement for you, you'll end up as fat as a house at this rate.

**Move the bike between your arms and legs**

# FRONT WHEEL LIFT

**B**efore we get started on this I want to tell you about a great place to practice these tricks. Empty car parks are perfect training grounds, and on any given Sunday most are empty of those annoying cars that get in the way. The reason they are so good; well they have built in markers (white lines) that help you gauge progress, create points to begin moves and basically assist in breaking down the move into manageable chunks. Lifting the front wheel is a great example of how your local (empty) car park can be a great training aid; check it out.

In your approach stance; start rolling towards a line on the floor and just lift the front wheel over it by compressing your arms slightly and then pulling up and back with your arms. Your weight will naturally come to the back of the bike and the front wheel will lift up. Practise this until you can confidently lift the front wheel over the line without touching it.

This sounds easy, and perhaps a little boring, but don't worry – 'from small acorns' and all that jazz. The progression from this move is to start using a kick of the pedal to help lift the wheel even higher, and with some confident control. To try this approach the line, then when a small distance from it put half a pedal stroke in so your weak foot leads as you hit

Go online and visit www.mtbtricks.co.uk for videos and tutorials

"
**DON'T BE SURPRISED IF YOU HAVE TO TAKE QUITE A FEW RUNS AT IT BEFORE THE TIMING BECOMES NATURAL**
"

the mark. What we are looking for here, is a clean action between your well practised lift, and a strong full-cycle of the cranks. The pedal action is the fuel to lift the wheel to a greater height than previous. The idea being; you control the power, thus control the lift. So the line is reached and you have the uncommon feeling of a weak foot leading the way, don't worry though. Just before the line begin that smooth pedal stroke I mentioned, and as the front wheel reaches the line you should be coming around onto your strong foot and coinciding its power with your lift as before. Imagine this line as a drop or step, this will help you time it correctly, but don't be surprised if you have to take quite a few runs at it before the timing becomes natural. The feeling is going to come from your visualisation of the move, so watch that podcast and let it sink in.

This move will also begin muscle development and synchronisation of your lifting action and pedal-stroke; something that will become ever more important as you become ever more awesome. As you improve it will be really tempting to start pedalling even more strokes, but be patient. We will get to the full blown wheelie in a short while, which will progress naturally from here. For now let's be satisfied with this and look at another important part of your bike, the rear wheel.

**Compress your arms and then pull**

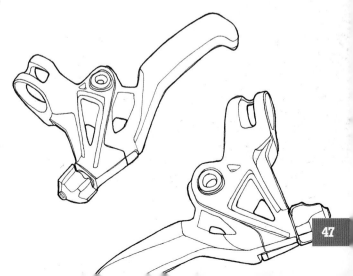

# REAR WHEEL LIFT

**O**K I admit our opening shot is another example of the extreme of this basic skill, don't be put off; I just want to illustrate the possibilities. The actual basic learning is far more achievable. Still in the car park (useful aren't they) let's start getting that back wheel off the ground. This is an important part of riding that can seem really daunting at first, especially if you have become accustomed to clip pedals and have now got to learn to lift that wheel without clips on. It really will be worth the effort though, because from this back wheel control you will find a doorway to all sorts of tricks and jumps. Popping a wheel over these white lines isn't glamorous but it will pay off.

**The white line has now morphed from a drop into a small log or rock; it's basically become an object that you want your rear wheel to clear without touching (or you'll be electrocuted and die! = incentive). So approach the lines and roll over the line and at first just try and sight when your rear wheel goes over.**

When you're happy with the timing involved have a go at lifting that wheel. It is a strange technique at first, almost certainly won't feel natural, but here is what it involves. The action of lifting comes from a more prominent feeling of pinning the bike between your hands and feet. Then manipulating the rear wheel into the air by pushing forward in a sharp quick movement with your weight, backwards and up with your feet – written down it's confusing, in reality it will soon click into effect. Concentrate on holding the bars and really feel your thumbs pulling around and under the bar to make the movement. Imagine trying to show yourself your palms without letting go (obviously). Your feet aren't attached so they hold the pedal by pushing down and back, your toes almost hooking over

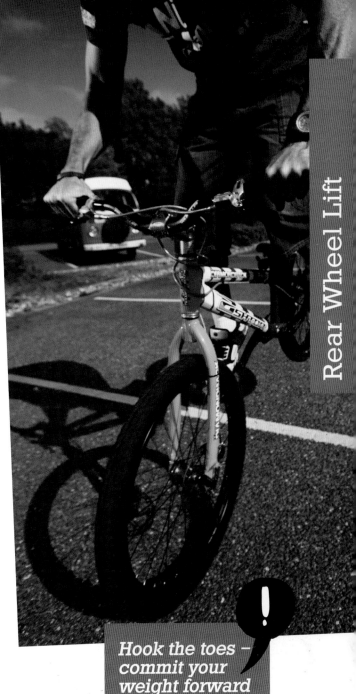

> ## *THIS IS AN IMPORTANT PART OF RIDING THAT CAN SEEM REALLY DAUNTING AT FIRST*

the front edge of the pedals. The result of hands and feet working will be the back wheel hopping off the ground. Simple really, from here it is just a matter of getting used to timing this lift with the white lines on the ground. Try and get some moderate speed and see how many lines you can successfully clear (one by one) in a row. The spacing between is small so if it's daunting at first just try every other line. This repetition will give you confidence and get the move firmly into your mind. Again we are also working on muscle memory here. Lifting both the front and rear wheels are bringing into play muscle groups that will work together when we get into the serious action. You've only gone and got loads better on that bike already!

**Hook the toes – commit your weight forward**

51

# BUNNY HOP

**T**he Bunny Hop is probably one of the difficult tricks to understand if you haven't ridden much before. If you've learnt it already, using clip pedals or toe clips then this is a time to discard them and learn the technique of bunny hopping correctly. The move itself seems basic enough but mastering it, even if it is only getting off the ground by millimetres, will enable you to take on so many other moves, some literally begin with a bunny hop, others just require the rider to have an understanding of control that bunny hopping requires, in short, it is a very useful move.

Go online and visit www.mtbtricks.co.uk for videos and tutorials

**Again an empty car park is ideal because we can use the lines as an imaginary obstacle right away. Strangely though... I'm going to ask you to find a small stick/plank that will turn our lovely flat area into a bunny-hop training zone.**

The piece of wood in question needs to be only a few centimetres in height. Enough to feel a bump as you ride over it. So place the plank on the floor and just simply ride over it several times. This is just a process to get the timing of your wheel spacing into your head, try it at different speeds too. Now start to use the plank as a small ramp for your front wheel. So approach the plank at a steady pace and go through the same front-wheel-lift process as you did earlier. Don't try and pedal, just go through it as before, several times. As you become more relaxed doing this, it will be easier to think about what is happening with the bike, so try and notice once you have lifted when the back wheel hits the plank. Don't worry about linking the two just yet, but let's move onto just the rear wheel now. So, approach with moderate speed, letting the front wheel just bump over, again trying to notice the timing as the back wheel hits. After going through this simple process a number of times try using that hit as a small lift to bring the rear wheel into the air. We don't need to break records, just get used to that feeling of the plank assisting your rear wheel lift.

We are getting close now to you pulling your first Bunny Hop. Your trail riding ability, and horizon for new techniques is about to take a huge jump forwards; let's do it.

Ride at the plank, again with moderate speed and in your approach position. What we want to achieve is both the processes from before, front and rear wheels coming off the ground. As the front wheel hits the plank, pull back as normal but keep your weight committed to the rear of the bike rather than letting the front drop down. Hopefully in not too many goes you will be able to do this long enough for the rear to hit the plank before the front has dropped. When that happens, forget about holding the front up and let the back ramp up into the air, just like it did earlier. In doing this you will have naturally forced the front wheel down, the effect will have been a donkey-kick motion (in fact 'donkey kick' is another well known name for the

# "

## *YOUR TRAIL RIDING ABILITY, AND HORIZON FOR NEW TECHNIQUES IS ABOUT TO TAKE A HUGE JUMP FORWARDS*

# "

# "CONCENTRATE ON KEEPING IT SMOOTH AND LANDING DOWN WITH CONTROL"

bunny hop). The front wheel up, then the hit of the rear wheel sends it into the air as well, although the front is dropping; importantly though, for a short moment, both wheels are off the ground. Rather than soaring into the sky like a young American child with a short space man in his shopping basket, let the bike drop back to the ground with control. You just bunny hopped! It may have felt like doing a small jump off a plank acting like a ramp, but it wasn't it was your first bunny hop. All that is left to do now (before you break the world high jump record: 1.32m at time of writing) is practise; oh, and lose the plank as assistance after a while. This may seem daunting, but don't worry about it. That will actually be a very natural process, but it will come after you have the sequence of hitting the plank dialled in. So don't rush, just enjoy perfecting that plank. Concentrate on keeping it smooth and landing down with control. The moment of 'air' will become more obvious as you improve, try holding the front end up and getting the back end down first, literally

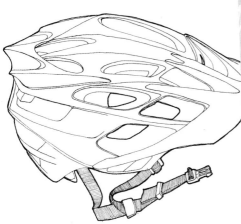

forcing it down with your legs, before your front wheel can drop. This will again improve your hop, and give you control that will pay dividends when we start looking at jumping.

Once this is a natural feeling, give the whole process another run through, only using just a line instead of a plank, it will feel awkward all over again, but you will soon find that it works just the same, and a true controlled bunny hop will drop neatly into your trick bag.

**Note:** The art of a bunny hop is to be able to get both wheels off the ground without a ramp. The reality of its use on the trail is getting some air from very minimal ramps, kickers or roots. Don't get too hung up on whether you are assisted by the plank, this is all teaching muscles to work together and create a new technique.

*Twist those hands and curl those toes!*

# RIDING DOWN STEPS

**M**y home town of Newbury is littered with subways and I used to spend an awful lot of time on steps, practising different riding skills. This urban furniture is such a useful piece of training equipment I just can't tell you. However before we start firing down them at break-neck speed, we should first consider some (probably obvious) safety thoughts. Riding down steps is dangerous for you, if you crash, it will really hurt and something could break – on the bike or on you. Riding down steps when other people are on them also; very bad idea, you could break them – as well as you. Lastly: riding down steps, when you don't know if anyone else is on them (or about to be) is a sure fire way of getting biking a bad name and breaking parts of you, the unfortunate passer-by, and unbelievably, most unacceptably your bike!

<blockquote>
**THE SECRET IS TO START SMALL AND GAIN CONFIDENCE IN THE SENSATION OF ROLLING OVER THE TOP**
</blockquote>

**Clearly your step riding venue must be well thought out. Look for a set that is short to begin, maybe just four or five steps and in a quiet area with good vision of the traffic that is likely to use them. If the perfect set of steps is quite busy, consider at what time they will be quiet. If it means making a special trip early in the morning, or leaving a riding session until evening then so be it, you will learn so much from these steps that it will be worth it.**

**Note:** it isn't legal to ride footpaths and steps; you need to be very careful about this. I spend most of my riding time on footpaths and urban furniture, and the best way of riding in these areas, with minimal fuss, is be courteous to anyone who is nearby or passing. Say "Hi" and smile, wait until they are safely passed before you continue to use the area, if that

means you never ride because you are always waiting for people to pass by - then ask yourself if this is the right place? If the worst happens and someone takes offence then take it on the chin, apologise, explain what you are doing and most importantly move on to somewhere else. Don't battle for your right to ride these steps, wall or footpath, you don't have that right. Courtesy of other users and a friendly smile can grant you permission though.

Perfect set of steps and time to ride them identified: OK we want to learn some important things on these steps. Things like; good bike control as we roll over the top, relaxed position as we are juggled around riding down them; an awareness of the angle we are riding, and how it effects our riding position. Most importantly though, we are going to face the fear of actually doing it; if you aren't used to riding this type of obstacle it will be very scary stuff. The secret is to start small and gain confidence in the sensation of rolling over the top. Start small, even a curb will work to begin, look for a double step, then a triple. Don't rush the process, owning this book doesn't teach you anything, reading it will.

Go online and visit www.mtbtricks.co.uk for videos and tutorials

Rolling over the top is the most important aspect to get right, if this early part of the move is controlled you are likely to ride out the bottom of the steps in good shape. Too much speed or not enough at the beginning and it could be A&E for you. So approach the steps at just more than walking pace, enough speed so you aren't correcting your balance with big turns of the front wheel. Letting the front wheel roll over the top steps and down will commit the bike into the move so it is important to learn the step mantra at this point 'front over the top, no chance to stop'. Basically once that front wheel has gone over you will feel the bike pulled over, attempting to back out now is futile because the effort to stop it now is a harder process to learn than just rolling down them. If you aren't sure then don't let that front over the top, but you can do it, so let's get on with it.

## HEAVY USE OF THE FRONT BRAKE WILL END IN TEARS, SO GENTLY DOES IT!

There's a rule that must be remembered, it's key to your success, 'keep your weight back'. This simple rule goes for any descent, that's all a set of steps are, just a very bumpy descent. This form of holding your weight back should be a controlled process that is timed with your bike entering into the steps as the front goes over. So look to start move backwards as the front enters and plan to be in the final position (see picture), with your bum right back once the back wheel is into the descent. From there it is just a case of letting the bike roll down and out of the obstacle; cover your brakes all the time. After a few goes try slowing the bike down on the steps, only slightly, but it is good to feel how the braking changes the sensation of riding down the steps. Heavy use of the front brake will end in tears, so gently does it!

**Let that bike do the work just roll down relaxed – weight back**

"My favorite aspect of racing is the adrenalin I get ripping it down the course faster than any other girl. There's only one thing that tops all that though... beating the boys!"

**Rachel Atherton**
2008 World Mountain Bike Downhill Champion

# ADVEN-TUROUS RIDING

In this next section you'll learn the skills that will form a basis for all that follows – but don't get me wrong, these aren't basic moves, you moved on from that the moment you started giving attention to your bike set-up and front-foot. No these moves are the stand alone impressive moves that are also the 'ground work' for very advanced riding – a bridge to the truly impressive stuff. The must have moves that will transform you from confident rider into an adventurous riding freak. These skills will come into effect on both trail and street riding. This is the part where you start to stick out from the crowd as a talented bike rider.

# TRACK STAND

**D**eveloping balance on your bike is essentially what this book is about. Obviously to nail any trick or move on a bike you must remain in control of the bike, to be in control you must be balanced. The track stand is what we call the art of balancing your bike whilst you are stationary. This move at first glance appears to be unrewarding, after all how much fun can you have on a bike when it isn't moving? Well I admit it's not glamorous but perfecting this move will make you a 110% better rider than before you could do it, you will also soar with confidence. I see it as a similar move to learning to stand up on a surf board; because that's how limited your riding is until you have balance and confidence. Lying on a surf board is fun, it can look cool but you're not experiencing surfing until you learn to stand up. With bikes you'll never experience all the fun stuff until you gain sufficient control through balance.

When I started practising for Trials competitions I was around 11 years of age. All my competitors had it nailed and I was desperate to learn it. I practised and practised, waiting for the skill to visit me but no matter how hard I battled the bike I would always topple over, I just couldn't hold the bike up right. After weeks of disappointment I eventually found balance. It came, and only visited me once I started to relax. Just look at that drop. I'm holding my balance but even though I'm in a dangerous position it's easy for me to remain calm and in control. That is because that calm balance is exactly the thing that will stop me from falling in the first place.

Your path to this nirvana of balance will come right outside your front door, next to a curb. Place your front wheel against a curb, slightly turned in towards the path, front brake on and front foot forward. You'll find it's possible to stand up on the pedals with the bike fixed in position as long as you keep that front brake fixed on.

Gently release the brake so you sense some movement, but quickly re-apply it. Depending on where your balance was, the front wheel will have turned slightly towards the curb or away. From that simple action you should become aware that you counter balance the bike's swing with an opposite reaction.

Now keeping the brake you will have found the only way to stay up in this fixed position is by leaning weight emphasis towards the curb – effectively leaning on it. Start to tease your weight away into the road and then return it before you go all the way. Subtle changes in weight distribution will have a big effect.

This rocking back and forth is the basis of the Trackstand. The next place to try it is on some soft terrain where you can go through the same process but with the front wheel in a small dip or bowl in the ground – which you'll be able to make with your foot. You're already track-standing now and it's just a matter of experimenting with it. Eventually you'll be able to happily stop and re-create this rocking motion on completely flat ground balancing by using a combination of brakes and pedals against each other.

The best way to get the rocking motion from the pedals is to practise on a grass slope and slowly ride up it, so slow that you come to a stop with your front foot forward. Let the weight of the bike hang on your strong front foot and the bike will rock. Before you roll backwards any distance, apply pressure again and ride away. Keep doing it until it feels natural. Try using the front brake as you did against the curb when you re-apply pressure on the pedals. Then release and try to let the bike come back down the hill controlled on your pedal. To and fro, back and forth between the pedal and brake is what you're after.

The Trackstand is a move that will create huge confidence in everything from here on in. Give it the time it deserves and try not to get frustrated with it – the simple steps will make it easier and once you've learnt it that technique will never leave you.

*Stay central over the bike and keep concentrated on a fixed point*

# POWER SLIDE & SKID CONTROL

**T**he Power Slide, amazing fun and so useful I just can't tell you. The name is a little misleading really, this skid doesn't increase speed or make you go faster. I am not sure of the origin of this name, I didn't come up with it but I think it relates to the sensation it gives, the back wheel steps out similar to how it would on a motorcycle that is powered into a turn. The Power Slide is a skid that is controlled to step out to the outside of a turn, allowing a new line into the turn to be created. To perfect it you need to spend hours riding fast downhill courses with tight single track corners that require the rider to change direction rapidly. In short the Power Slide is a very technical move but essentially begins with learning to skid, so let us start with that.

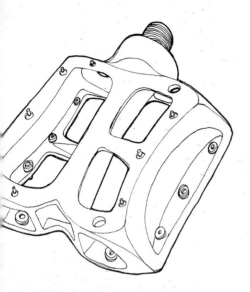

### Start with some skidding:

This simple technique is well known and can seem like a rather useless trick, or no more than over zealous braking. In truth it's also the beginnings of brake control, because to find out how much braking is too much, you have to apply the brake fully until it locks, and then skid when you hold the brake on. Let me be clear that I'm only talking about the rear brake here, experimenting with heavy use of the front brake will lead to an accident for sure. We will come to front brake control later.

I want to get across to you how much fun skidding is, and the control you gain from learning it is basically a win/win situation.

Your practice area should be an open bit of trail on level or slightly descending ground, be aware that stopping time will increase with a slight descent, non existent on a steep descent. At first practise with space that means you can let the brake off and roll before you reach a real need to stop, for example; don't practise into a corner yet, near a drop or even a road. Once you

Go online and visit www.mtbtricks.co.uk for videos and tutorials

have the location sorted start by riding along with pace, and then roll along with your front foot forwards. Apply the rear brake, hard for just a few moments, this will help you anticipate the feeling of it in the future, note that the braking effect will differ wildly on different terrain. Once you have investigated this feeling start to hold it longer and longer until eventually the bike is skidding all the way to a complete stop. Continue to play with it, moving your body weight back and forth so you can feel that the more weight over the rear will make it harder to skid. Similarly weight over the front will let the rear snake around behind you easily. This balance of weight is what will help you control skidding into corners as you become more experienced. For now play with it, and start to use it on the trail or even on your 8-Track.

Make sure that the practice area isn't concrete or tarmac else you will ruin the tyre in no time, also try to use an area that is rough enough not to be ruined by skid marks, sure the ground will heal but you don't want the village hall attacking you for defacing the local green with skid marks.

## " I WANT TO GET ACROSS TO YOU HOW MUCH FUN SKIDDING IS "

### Now for some Power Sliding:

The skid is now a natural feeling, hopefully you may even hacked around your 8-Track so much that it has some cool skid ruts into the corner. Now that you are using it into corners the powerslide is an option, in MotoGP terms we are thinking about 'backing it in'. The idea is using a skid to scrub off speed and alter your line into a corner or approach to an obstacle. The trick is balancing how much you speed you lose and how much direction change it results in, here lies the difficulty in getting this move right. Again practice will be your only way to get better and the mantra should help you approach do that. The Power Slide will only work when you are approaching a corner with excessive speed, this is why it's dangerous and difficult, and exciting! When you can use the power-slide to scrub off pace and improve your angle of entry into the corner, then you have it nailed. The skid needs to finish before you hit the apex of the corner, also before you lose too much speed. How much speed is too much? Well rest assured, approaching any corner at the rate of a top downhill rider like World Champion Gee Atherton is going to be too much, the artistry of riders like Gee is just how little they brake and how much speed they dare carry through the corners, what they achieve is staggering, and unfortunately can't be taught in this book, you either have that or you don't. Putting the Power Slide to good use on the trails is achievable though so get practising. Remember that you are aiming

> ## "THIS ONLY WORKS WHEN YOU ARE APPROACHING A CORNER WITH EXCESSIVE SPEED, THIS IS WHY IT'S DANGEROUS AND EXCITING!"

to carry speed through the corner, if you are losing too much speed then you're still skidding, and missing out the 'power'. To gain confidence approaching with your inside foot out as a stabiliser, this will also place your outside foot at the bottom of the pedal stroke and keep your weight in the optimum place during the turn. Don't try to get back on the pedal until you're through the corner though. One thing to remember with any cornering technique; it is very important to practise it both left and right. One direction will seem slightly awkward but this goes in very little time if you persevere. Don't be frightened of opposite lock.

**Weight forward and stabilise with inside leg – have confidence to steer**

# THE WHEELIE

**T**he wheelie is such a simple trick that everyone recognises. In the Bike Trick category, it would be the top answer on Family Fortunes when Vernon utters the immortal words 'the survey says'. The wheelie is so popular for a very good reason, it's so much fun. There's no trick more rewarding; the feeling of controlling a wheelie is awesome and addictive. Once you've learnt the wheelie, you will have a trail weapon of serious effect, a show boating 'party piece' that pleases all and most importantly a move dialled that will make in-roads into becoming a very technically proficient bike rider.

It isn't a trick that will be learnt in a 10 minute session though, it is something to approach in stages but you will pleased to know that you have already taken some of those stages on already, you're well on the way to nailing this.

Look for a grassy area to learn the basics, because it is likely you will take a few spills on the way to getting this right 'you can't make an omelette without cracking some eggs!' so don't worry about the tumbles, just choose a spot that will be forgiving when you have to jump off the back and then it won't matter (your eggs will be safe).

Start by making a small change to your bike; raise the seat up by a few inches because we are going to learn this trick sitting down. Also place a marker of some kind on the ground as a 'begin' point so you have a reference of where to start. It can be anything, a stick or a scuff in the grass; keep using this point as your 'begin' because it will help you set up properly on each attempt.

Approach at a gentle pace and in a gear that has some torque left at this speed; by this I mean you shouldn't be in a gear that has no effect when you pedal at this speed. Your gear choice should give you a quick and comfortable acceleration, without huge effort when you put the power down; remember you are the engine of the bike; your legs are literally the motor that powers this machine.

Your riding position should be sitting on the high seat position with arms flexed and your front foot forward. As you reach your marker compress your arms slightly, then pull back letting your arms lock out, and then flex again as you pull up and pedal in sync. Just concentrate on giving three pedals to start with; by this I mean one push with your front foot, then a second push with your weak, finishing with a third from your strong. Experiment with this process a bit, this will be a strange feeling and getting the timing right is going to take a few goes but it will start to make sense quite quickly. Don't get down hearted if it doesn't feel like an awesome controlled wheelie yet, it will. This trick has been learnt by literally millions of people, you are going to be the next.

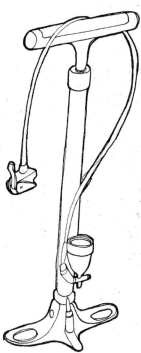

Now that is working we need to get you used to committing your weight far enough back to get a wheelie going. We do this in two ways: firstly go through the process from before but power so much that you have to step off the back of the bike, literally go so steep that you end up standing behind the bike walking along to stop it. Now as you step off the back grab the rear brake and notice how the handle bars pull on your arms, the back brake pulls the front end down. By doing this we have discovered that you have an escape route and the back brake has an important effect on the control options of the wheelie. The skills you need to wheelie are all revealed to you; it is a combination of power, commitment of weight to the rear and balance of both those things via the rear brake.

Now ride at your marker and power the wheelie up, do your three pedals as in the beginning (should be comfortable with getting it high now) and as you get to the third pedal – hopefully still increasing in height – apply the rear brake and stop powering, the front wheel should be pulled downwards to the floor. Get this mantra of pedal/brake into your head, practise will make perfect and you need to put some time into getting this right. Remember: your rear brake is the control and you have an escape route 'out the back door'. Be confident and ride at this move with a determined attitude, other wise it won't happen. Confidence is key and taking your time to understand the how and why this move works is important.

Go online and visit www.mtbtricks.co.uk for videos and tutorials

Now that you are happy with the pedal/brake system; we just need to link it together. On this approach hit the brake as normal but before the front end can touch down start another three pedals, try and pull with the arms, power with the pedals back up into the braking point again. This is essentially the wheelie nailed, because you now just need to develop that sequence into a smooth process.

**Top Tips for wheelie good success!**

At the start I told you to ride at this on a high seat; which you should but if you are very new to this then run through that first process of the lift with the seat very low; this will make it nearly impossible to get and front wheel height, so it's safe and you can get used to the powering of the pedals. Slowly raise the seat in stages to start feeling the difference in weight distribution. The higher the seat, the quicker your weight will be over the rear wheel when you pull up. Don't go too high with the seat though, you could get tangled up in it when trying to step off the back later in the learning.

The side-ways balance of the wheelie is important too, but will be an obvious technique as you learn. The bike needs to move between your knees from side to side, these gentle movements come from movements in the handle bars from your flexed arms. Gentle steering from left to right is how to control it. Remember the wheelie is a combination of balancing the rearwards' weight pushed by the pedal power, and the opposite effect of the rear brake pushing the front wheel back down.

Stay relaxed, mean it, enjoy it!

**Be brave: find that balance point and you have it in the bag**

# SIDE BUNNY HOP

**W**hen I think about the Side Bunny Hop I don't really capture images of a hugely impressive trick. It isn't steeped in riding history or likely to win the hearts of adoring bike fans; in fact it isn't really a standalone trick at all. I'm really talking about developing your existing Bunny Hop skills into a truly useable trail riding trick that can get you out of trouble. So if you like, we can think of this section as an extension to the Bunny Hop learning process, a natural progression to absolute control over a move, giving you awesome trail confidence.

> # THIS MOVE IS ABOUT HAVING CONTROL AND CONFIDENCE IN YOUR ABILITY TO PLACE THE BIKE WHERE YOU WANT

I remember being on a photo shoot with multiple World Cup champion Steve Peat one time. A moment arose that captured this move, its simplicity and usefulness that I will never forget. We were moving along a trail at quite a pace, I was following Steve and enjoying the undulating route. Every now and then Stevie would put a burst of power down and I'd know there was a descent coming. Riding with a World class downhill racer, it is inevitable that you will have some pretty quick descents and I was enjoying it, if not struggling a little bit to keep up. This particular time I remember seeing Steve burst away with some cranks of the pedal so I did the same. The trail we were on was flat and running along the top of a tree strewn valley, it felt pretty high up. Ahead it was as though the trail ended, there was nothing but thick trees coming up and the burst of speed felt a bit out of

place, I knew Stevie knew the trail well though so I stepped on it. Then I noticed another trail was running along side us. It appeared like a new route on a train line, curving away from us sharply but then turning back instantly to run fast beside us. Now that I'd noticed it I could feel it snaking along next to us, it was slightly lower than our trail, and on the side of the drop into the valley. Steve had pulled ahead slightly (this happens a lot with Steve Peat) and so I had a great view of the move. As our Trail came to an end at the trees, Steve pulled on the bars, lifting the front wheel and turning it towards the parallel trail, un-weighting the bike the rear wheel came up and started to follow the front end across. Mid air across the gap Steve turned the bars opposite lock and started steering down the line of the other trail, still mid air. The back wheel now moved into line with the front and Stevie touched down on

the other trail just as it dropped away into the valley steeply, and he disappeared out of site. Later on, after that ride I remember thinking what a beautiful riding moment it was, I didn't think "Wow! Steve Peat has a great Side Bunny Hop." That isn't what this move is about; it's about having control and confidence in your ability to place the bike where you want, even if that place is two foot to the left (or right).

Go online and visit www.mtbtricks.co.uk for videos and tutorials

If you are still mastering the Bunny Hop itself, don't worry that this is too advanced. Just start adding this into your practice. It will raise your horizon regarding the move and you will progress quicker. Use a stick on the floor or a marker to help you visualize the beginning of the move, timing is everything. The Bunny Hopping process, the bit that will get the wheels off the ground, is exactly the same as before. This time though, as the front end comes up begin steering towards the side you want to go. Your outside hand (if you're going left, your right hand) will have emphasis over the other as you pull on the bars to lift the rear wheel. This pull is going to naturally straighten the handle bars out. If we froze frame now, you would be at a slight angle between the two lines, handlebars straight. Thankfully we are in a fluid movement, not a scene from The

"

## DON'T BE SURPRISED OR DISAPPOINTED IF AT FIRST YOU KEEP CHANGING DIRECTION BUT NOT LANDING PARALLEL

"

Matrix, so now let the emphasis on your pull from one side, turn into a push from the other bringing the front end down towards the landing and turning the bars in the direction you wish to land. The back wheel will follow you across. Don't be surprised or disappointed if at first you keep changing direction but not landing parallel. This is just as useful a move because no two trails are the same, on a certain route you may need exactly this. What is important is you are changing direction with a Bunny Hop. To get the parallel landing you must really pull hard on the bars, giving time for the opposite push, and then really commit your legs to bringing the back end over into line with your desired route.

Once you have this trick dialled it will be so useful and the term side bunny hop will fade. The name doesn't stick or conjure a certain trick because it's such a versatile move. We start with a Side Bunny Hop, but finish with a whole lot more than that.

*Front wheel first – will bring the back-end in line*

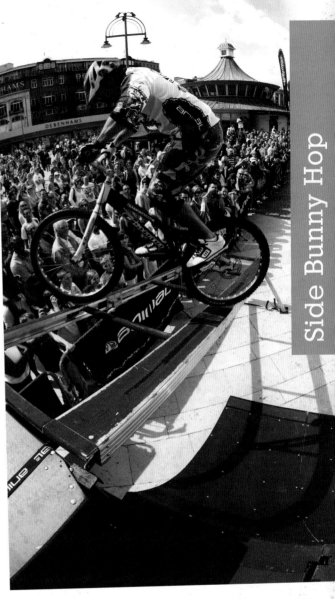

# WHEELIE
# DROP OFF

The wheelie drop off is just like the side-bunny hop in the sense that it's further development of a previous move you have already learned, the wheelie. What's really great about this move though, is you don't have to learn more technique. Actually we could change the name to 'wheelie timing' because that's really what we will be talking about. We will again be learning a move that we can call by a single name but it will lead to many more uses that that name suggests. This is where we begin to put that 'show boating' wheelie into action, riding off, over and up obstacles that seemed impossible when you first picked up this book. Let's start with riding off a drop, the 'up' and 'over' will come later.

My earliest memory of doing a big wheelie drop-off was way back when I was at school. I used to ride to school at a time when mountain bikes were new and becoming fashionable and 'road racer' styled bikes were popular, my BMX was not. I loved it though because I spent all my spare time pretending it was my Trials motorbike, that I rode at weekends (Trials pushbikes were only just getting discovered by a small group of Essex based bikers whilst away in Spain). So my BMX had to get me to school and back, as well as be my mid-week training device.

My school routes led me past a small children's play area, called the Spider Park. A wall surrounding the Spider Park only stood two feet high at the path but dropped about five feet down into the play

> **"**
>
> **I DECIDED TO GO FOR IT BECAUSE SOME MATES WERE EGGING ME ON RATHER THAN CONFIDENCE IN MY ABILITY**
>
> **"**

area that was sunken into the ground. At one particular point where the path approached this wall, the bricks had been knocked away, leaving just the tiniest ridge of remaining wall cement (maybe 3cm high) and then the five foot drop into the park. On my way to school each day I would look at this drop as I approached it along the path, then turn away as the route snaked me around the Park. For some reason on my return journey one day I stopped to investigate it further. If I decided to ride off this drop I would need to time the wheelie perfectly because the braking systems of today were not present on my beat-up old Raleigh Burner. I probably decided to go for it because some mates were egging me on rather than confidence in my ability. Even now though, I can remember thinking how I used the small concrete lip to time the drop. Lifting the front wheel as it hit, then timing my weight distribution and pedal stroke to propel the back wheel up the small bump, and then off the rather large drop. Five feet later I had landed my first big drop-off and snapped my first pair of cheap handlebars. Thankfully manufacturing techniques of handlebars have improved and the technique to wheelie drops is still as good now as it was back then. It goes a little something like this.

Let's use the plank as a marker again; it will work exactly like the cement I used all that time ago. Like the Bunny Hop and other techniques where we have used a plank like this; learn with it and the discard once you have progressed and ready for some proper big drop-offs!

Place the plank at the edge of a curb. This curb is our five foot high drop; this will require some imagination but remember the technique at the top of a thirty metre drop is exactly the same as that on a curb like this.

Approaching the drop will mean you are rolling on your front foot, but about two bike lengths away pedal round onto your opposite foot. As the front wheel hits the plank lift the front just like a wheelie, with power coming from a complete pedal stroke (weak foot around to strong foot). This process will bring your back wheel up the plank which you will feel it as a slight bump, you will also know from that feeling that the drop is about to happen. At this point the front should be high and out over the drop, your pedal stroke should be complete and the back brake should be covered so you can feather it for wheelie control if needed. On slow speed drops you may need a small kick of the pedal again to propel you off at a good angle. Either way it is important to stop your pedal stroke as your back wheel is at the edge; off a curb it won't seem that important for your front foot to lead, but as the drop-offs get bigger it will become very important for your landing.

The drop position itself is flexed arms and knees, ready for compression on landing. This landing will be dependant on your position as you left the edge, but it should be a back wheel first landing and in control. Front too low and it will be uncomfortable at small height 'Bike Snapping' off a big drop. Too steep an angle with the front wheel too high will result in looping out off the curb, leading to some serious bum bruising off anything bigger. The important thing to remember with drop-offs is to take your time and learn at a height that is fine to make mistakes on. As your t____ ____es you will n___ ____ _____d at this s___gc y___ ____ _____ _rops will ___ ____ the__ ____ __ be looking at them ___ ____ __ _rom going too big, to_ ____ possible to just roll off drops a__ ___st using your

> ## "
> # THE DROP POSITION ITSELF IS FLEXED ARMS AND KNEES, READY FOR COMPRESSION ON LANDING
> "

momentum rather than 'pedal powered' control but that technique is harder to judge. Unless you have great manual-wheelie control (will learn later) let's stick with this technique that will teach timing for other techniques we have coming up like 'riding up an obstacle'. So let things progress in this controlled manner and once you have learned the manual at a later date, then apply it to drop-offs.

> **Be on that strong front-foot as the back wheel reaches the edge – then kick**

"I've travelled around the World and seen some amazing things through my riding career. I never set-out with that intention, I was simply enjoying my bike and luckily people seemed to like what I did with it. I'm certainly enjoying the 'whole' ride now!"

**Grant 'Chopper' Fielder**
International Dirt Jump star

# GETTING
# RAD

In this section we will learn to control 'air time' and develop Jump skills that will lead to awesome tricks. Learning to jump is fun and on some trails necessary. The tricks are completely unnecessary on the trail, but if you want to impress your mates then this is the place where you will find techniques to set you apart from the rest.

# TAKE OFF AND LANDING

**Y**ou can't have one without the other, but let's take it one step at a time and start at the beginning. Taking off is the first major step in the process, you will find that landing comes naturally thanks to gravity; however we want that natural result to be one that is smooth and controlled. I've said it many times already but confidence will be an important key to success when learning to jump. I think the way to earn that confidence (because that's what you do) is to start small and work your way up – literally.

# THERE ARE MANY TYPES OF JUMP EVERY SINGLE ONE CAN FEEL COMPLETELY DIFFERENT

I've seen it so many times: at bike trails, jump spots and BMX track; a rider turns up who is clearly new to riding, or new to ramps and jumps. The first thing this rider does is start hitting the ramps at speed. This 'newbee' is simply experimenting with the process of getting some air, trying different speeds – usually starting slow and getting faster and faster until he/she eventually takes off. I've seen this many times, in fact if you go to your local jump spot you will probably see it nearly everyday. One thing I have never seen when these aspiring jump riders get their first taste of air: the divine gift of instant jump prowess! Why would you suddenly be able to handle this new situation when only moments ago you were experimenting with the very ordinary process of going over a bump at speed, wheels on the ground! Now you are three feet off it and for some reason the back wheel is trying to overtake you by passing over your head!

Make a decision now to not be that person; let's start small - boring even – and get the result we intended in the first place. If not you'll end up scared with a lifelong memory of the day you smashed your teeth out, taking an opinion to your grave that "bikes aren't really for me". They are, and you can get really good on them too!

Our first location for learning to take off needs to be very subtle, you have already begun the process when you started to bunny hop. I'm sure whilst doing that you decided to hit that plank at some pretty excessive speeds, and when doing that you began to learn to jump. Now we need to move on from the plank and find a natural bump or bank that will allow us to get a bit of air as safely as possible.

Make sure you bring the seat down so it's out of the way and always approach the take off with your momentum created in plenty of time, comfortably in your approach position.

The aim here is to get used to the feeling of how different the bike feels – and your weight distribution changes when you hit a bump like this at speed. You will feel the bike comes up towards you. As you continue to experiment with this bump try to notice how your take off position affects the actual jump and landing. As early as possible, try to get the timing similar to the bunny hop. Take off front wheel first, as the rear wheel leaves let the bike come up towards you but try and force the back end down to the ground as landing approaches, touching down before the front wheel.

There are many types of jump. Every single one can feel completely different and it's good to know that each new jump requires a certain amount of learning. It is not common for any rider to hit a jump first time at full speed and nail it perfect. Most riders will build up to it - just like you have on this bump – and get comfortable with the ramp and landing, how much speed is needed to clear it etc.

So this bump has opened your thoughts to jump riding; time to hit the local spot (see 'Great places to ride and chat' section if unsure) and start experimenting. As mentioned at the start of this book; I'm not going to get bogged down with every detail of technique, just getting you started and interested in each move, then visualising it through the online videos will be enough, the rest is just experimentation – with hopefully more knowledge, inspiration and safety than if you'd never bought this book.

Start small and let the confidence grow – as it does so will your jumps

# STYLE; START MOVING THAT BIKE AROUND

I'm hoping by now that you have found a great place to practise jumps. It really should be at a local skate park or jump trails. I know I have bored you with safety in this section so far, but jumps can lead to big injuries (I have big scars and bumpy bones to prove it) so get the location right. Basically you're looking for a place where there are other riders jumping; this brings safety in case of accidents, and friends who can help and guide you in learning. I will talk more about it later but those spotty kids, or angry looking jump experts are actually very friendly and want nothing more than to see you flying with confidence. OK no more safety it is time to start getting some style into your jumps.

Go online and visit www.mtbtricks.co.uk for videos and tutorials

**Way back in the mid-nineties a rider emerged in the magazines called Steve Geal. Steve was from a BMX background but in the world of MTB that I was involved he was a new face. He hit the scene with force, turning up at big events and breaking the world Bunny Hop record with ease; his technique was awesome and effortless. I was blown away by his riding (still am) but it wasn't until I saw him on jumps that I realised how good he was.**

When Steve 'Gilly' Geal jumps it looks amazing, so smooth and he seems to be able to put the bike anywhere he wants, unfortunately – and awkwardly considering I'm teaching you here – I don't jump as well and I can't just put the bike anywhere I want! Don't panic though, I can jump; I can do all the show stuff like Back-Flips and everything, which we will look at later. However this part of the book is more about style than actual tricks, and that ease comes from doing jumps all the time, getting as confident in the air as you are on the ground. We want to grasp that ease that made Gilly look so good (literally WE – me and you). That ease is going to take practise, to progress on from here you will need to dedicate a lot of time to

# "THE SECRET TO GETTING AIR-TIME COMFORT IS TO FOCUS AT AN EARLY STAGE ON LANDING"

riding jumps. The basics are exactly what they say they are, basic. Getting some style is personal and – excitingly I think – quite random because you will be led by who you see and what you like. With that in mind I can't very well start breaking this down into a solid technique. This is experimentation and self learning and will decide what else in the book appeals to you, especially as you learn more jumps.

The secret to getting air-time comfort is to focus at an early stage on landing. On a jump box, that has a nice big landing start trying to clear the box and land both wheels at the same time - done by adjusting your position in the air. If the rear wheel is hitting along time before the front then your weight is too far back, front coming in to steep then you've gone to far forward. Learning this balancing of the bike in the air is beginning to teach you to move the bike around.

> ## "
> ## THERE IS NO CORRECT WAY, JUST WHAT SUITS YOU SO STICK WITH THAT TO BEGIN "

The next step is to start hitting the jump box at a slight angle, don't exaggerate this too much because I don't want you missing the landing ramp. To start just come across from one side; I suggest going across it from left to right if your front-foot is right like me, vice versa if left foot. Coming up the take off at this different angle will change the reaction you get from the ramp; it will feel less steep for instance. At the very beginning the change in the take-off ramp at this angle will be good as it will make you aware of the irregularity of ramps, demonstrating how just a small change can make it feel like a different ramp. Hitting it at this angle you want to take off and then steer mid air in the direction you wish to go, towards the

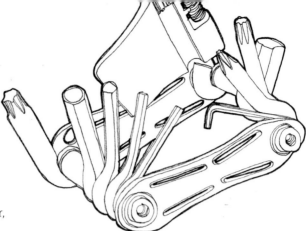

middle of the landing. When I say steer, I'm talking about your shoulders and weight committing you back towards the centre. Your bars will turn but it isn't them that are changing the direction, it's your body weight. There are ways to help this process such as deciding on a particular place to land or aim. This will mean you are looking for it after take-off and you will then naturally commit your weight towards it. Try and get comfortable with this turning motion in the air. You will find as you experiment that you can arc up the take-off slightly to exaggerate the move.

It will be clear very quickly that you have a comfortable direction to do this in, likely to be left to right for right footers as I mentioned, but that isn't definite by any means. There is no correct way, just what suits you so stick with that to begin. However try and practice it the other way as soon as you can, it will feel really alien compared to your strong direction but nailing this control will set you up for great control in the future. As I mentioned loads of times, all jumps are different and this technique will ensure you are moving the bike exactly where you want it. It also leads us handily onto some of the other basic moves when jump riding.

**Look for the landing spot and let your body steer the bike through the air**

# THE SCRUB:
## JUST KEEPING IT LOW

O K the scrub is actually not very basic, in fact it's a move that racers like Steve Peat or Gee Atherton spend ages practising. You're not going to perfect it after a few words from me; however we can use it as the inspiration for a very useful technique: keeping it low! This technique of 'soaking up' a jump is very useful for many reasons. In the beginning it is a great way of taking the fear out of a new trail for example. Self belief will grow from the knowledge that any jump can be flattened; this will have any rider attacking a new route with far more assertion. 'Keeping it low' is also a way of carrying speed; getting big air time and pulling tricks is one thing. If the goal is to beat a mate down a hill or around a track then this technique will make serious gains in lap times. Plenty of practice and experience in many different situations will mean you can pull this move off. In extreme cases the Scrub will mean you can keep the bike so low across the gap and over the peak of the landing that the bike is laid flat and skims over the surface of the trail. It is seriously fast and looks bloody amazing.

# THE TECHNIQUE OF 'SCRUBBING' A JUMP ORIGINATES FROM MOTOCROSS

"

"

I used to ride on one of the biggest mountain bike teams in the nineties called Volvo Cannondale. I was the Trials rider for the team and effectively not too important in the grand scale of things. Volvo Cannondale was glittered with top names in all the disciplines of mountain biking (including Trials – Me!). Brian Lopes was a member at one stage and I remember seeing the Multi-World BMX and 4X racing champion put on a master class of 'keeping it low' one particular day.

We were at a jump spot in California, the trails in question were pretty big and I was watching Brian and fellow Volvo Cannondale rider Cedric Garcia glide through them with ease, clearing the huge gaps with ease. After a great session these two racing geniuses got into a little contest of who could get through these huge

Go online and visit www.mtbtricks.co.uk for videos and tutorials

mounds of dirt the quickest. Cedric went first and the rapid Frenchman, known for his exciting personality and riding went so fast! I was actually stunned at his pace but he hadn't bargained on Brian's Motocross skills coming into play. The technique of 'Scrubbing' a jump originates from Motocross, and Brian Lopes does a lot of that in his spare time. He approached the trails with such aggression and speed I was expecting him to try and take off from the first jump and clear a huge gap, landing in the second jumps landing or something? However Brian sucked up all that momentum as he took off, forcing the bike low across the gap and maintaining the crazy pace into the second jump and subsequently through the entire run. He demonstrated perfect text book examples of keeping it low through the whole trail; eight huge jumps and two burmed corners can never have been ridden so fast, his

bike's wheels looked glued to the ground! It was clear at that moment how Mr Lopes had won so many BMX titles; a discipline of racing bikes that requires this technique all the time. It was an awesome display of riding talent and to witness one of the very best racers of all time in his element was a treat for me.

Depending on how you see it we don't need huge dirt jump trails in California to begin learning to keep it low. You were probably looking forward to the trip I know, but these were seriously big jumps and I think we should get it nailed on some more sedate examples first. So before you go and buy a plane ticket and pack your bike into a bag; find yourself a nice bump to play with – the one you used for 'take-offs' is perfect.

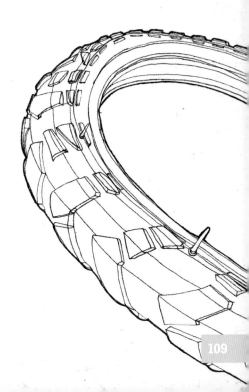

Start by rolling at the obstacle with medium pace in the approach position; go over it a few times without trying to jump or have speed enough to need to think about controlling air time, just quick enough to feel the bike follow the undulation and push you upwards at the peak of the bump. Start to increase the speed at which you do this until you are feeling the beginnings of the jump, maybe even do a couple of jumps to get the pace right. Once you are happy the pace is affecting the bike significantly (in that it's making you jump or wheels lift off) try soaking it up at the peak. You do this by letting your arms and legs compress as you go over the bump. The bike will follow the contour of the ground, but you should try and make your upper body remain fixed on a constant line of trajectory. Keep doing this until you are confidently eating up the forces created over this bump and then move it onto something a bit more challenging.

A jump box at your local skate park is a great place for advancing this move, or the table top jump at a BMX or 4X track is perfect. Basically something that has a clear take-off ramp and landing, that doesn't have to be cleared like a double. It goes without saying that you can't perfect 'keeping it low' until you can easily 'get it high'. Your chosen jump must be one that is a comfortable obstacle that you can jump normally with ease. Happy with the jump then start applying the same process as the bump. On the bump we tried to keep your body follow a flat trajectory but over this jump it will be impossible as the take off will naturally take you up and over. If you imagine your head leaving a light trail it would clearly go along then up and then down as you negotiate the jump. What we want to try and do is increase your speed over the jump but keep that arc

as low as possible. Force the bike towards the floor as you take off by letting your body soak it up through the arms and legs.

As you improve it will be obvious that attacking the jump at a faster and faster pace is going to result in you not being able to soak it up, and crashing. Before we get to that point start to experiment with turning the handle bars down and over to one side (probably away from your front foot, whatever feels comfortable). By doing this you should be able to get your body weight further over the front of the bike than if you kept the bars straight. It will be a similar line to the one you took when experimenting with moving the bike around in the air. Only this time you are trying to keep the bike as low as possible and maintain speed. Getting this right will also be a great time to get confidence with landing front wheel first. Something that we will use later in riding dirt jump trails.

Eat-up the jump with exaggerated compression – force the bike low

# TRAN-SITION RAMP DROP IN

In the last couple of techniques I have mentioned jump boxes and skate parks. Transitions are the ramps made from a section of circle and can also be known as Quarters (short for quarter pipe) or when it's two ramps facing each other a Half Pipe. Any skate park will be drizzled with this style of obstacle. Going up one of these ramps is one thing but 'dropping in' is often a far more challenging learning experience, especially if the transitions at your local park are quite big. Until recently many riders would have argued 'mountain biking doesn't belong in skate parks' (not many mountains and all that) but increasingly the lines between cycling disciplines of mountain biking and BMX have been blurred.

Nowadays one of the mountain bike's strengths is its versatility; a standard rigid (no suspension) mountain bike design can handle moderate riding on all terrains. Focused specialist designs have been created for all areas of riding including: downhill racing, which utilises advanced suspension technology; free riding bikes that are a mixture of cross country and downhill; and 4X and dirt jump bikes for use in 4X racing and on dirt-jump trails and skate parks.

Within all these disciplines there are deviations again that demonstrate the versatility of the genre that is mountain bikes. Trials riding, for example, has a whole scene that focuses on urban riding and the obstacles that location generate. A completely new design of mountain bike has stemmed from this 'street' scene - the 24-inch street bike - as ridden by Danny MacAskill. I must admit I've been an exponent of this new 24-inch wheeled 'street trials' revolution; releasing the first example of a design back in 2003. The versatility and adaptability of mountain biking can not be underestimated. Seeing MTB as a sport that is only about mild cross-country riding will only limit the terrain and experiences you encounter.

> ## *I CAN SYMPATHISE WITH ANY RIDER WHO LOOKS AT A TRANSITION RAMP WITH TREPIDATION*

So a skate/BMX park is a great place for you to enjoy your riding, you really don't need a skate board or a specific BMX, as I've mentioned, mountain bikes can go anywhere.

I can sympathise with any rider who looks at a transition ramp with trepidation. In the beginning of learning they are very tricky obstacles and an honest and sensible approach would be to have some fear, these things could mess you up! However don't be put off by that dramatic reality check, take it as a pointer to starting small and working your way up...or down if you see what I mean.

**115**

> ## THEY CALL IT VERT BECAUSE THE LAST FEW FEET OF THE TRANSITION LITERALLY IS A VERTICAL WALL!

Starting small didn't register on my radar as a young pro-rider in the early nineties. At that time mountain bikes were not seen on skate style ramps or parks. The sport was still very much developing and as a trials rider I was busy introducing Trials riding (along with a select few) as a form of mountain biking itself. At that time BMX riding was just coming out of a huge slump that ensued after the mid Eighties boom it had enjoyed. This far steadier growth in BMX came from freestyle riding, led by now legendary names such as Matt Hoffman and Dave Mirra. I had a few VHS tapes of these riders and watched them develop this form of riding in an incredible way. So when I came across my first really big transition ramp I was very keen to have a go. I wasn't necessarily aware of

Go online and visit www.mtbtricks.co.uk for videos and tutorials

the dangers. The ramp in question was a 14 foot high Vert half-pipe. It had steps that lead you from the back, up onto the deck (the surface at the top of the ramp). I remember looking down and thinking how crazy – and different – the prospect of dropping in was from this perspective. A Vert ramp is the biggest of transitions you will find in a park, it is not the ramp to attempt your first 'drop in' on. They call it Vert because the last few feet of the transition literally is a vertical wall! So at this stage of the story I will admit to some arrogance in ability that my Trials skills had given me. I was scared but completely confident that I could handle this situation, I would soon be rolling up and down this ramp just like Matt Hoffman. "Perhaps I will try a back flip after lunch!" You get the idea; and can probably guess how this is going to turn out. I rolled along the deck and attempted the 'drop in', the result was a very good example of the term known as hanging-up; something that happens when you haven't popped into the ramp in the correct way. To explain, the bike is straddled across the top lip of the ramp, front wheel pointing down and the rear hanging you there. The result is usually a fierce weight shift forwards as the bike slows quickly but your momentum is continuing. Hanging-up is possible to recover from on smaller transitions but the extremes of a Vert didn't help me. I basically went over the handle bars and down face first into the base of the Vert ramp, the bike then followed landing on top of a very bruised, battered and very winded body. I remember thinking as I lay there struggling for breath that I should have started on something smaller; I'd like to say I learnt immediately from the experience but as you read on in later chapters, you'll soon realise it took a few more injury experiences for it to hit home.

Hopefully that little story hasn't put you off and you're still keen to starting rolling in (see me smiling embarrassingly). I certainly don't mean to put you off; better you learn from my mistakes than repeat them though. Most skate parks will have plenty of different transitions to drop into but your first should be a mellow example, look for one that is no more than 3ft in height to begin. Importantly look for one that has enough deck on top that you can approach head on, rather than having to ride alongside the coping (top edge of the ramp) and then turn in ninety degrees to drop-in. We will look at that later but first we need to get you in safely and with confidence.

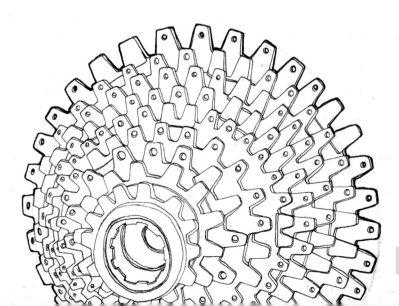

> ## "NAILING DROP-INS REQUIRES SOME CONFIDENCE IN YOUR BUNNY HOPPING TECHNIQUE "

Ramp identified: ride approach it at a slow pace, speed is not a friend of dropping-in.

At the height of ramp we have started at you will probably be able to just roll over the top and in no problem. This is a good idea but getting from top to bottom isn't rolling in, and any ramp of 4ft or more will prove that via a tumble over the bars. So by all means experiment with just rolling in at first but when it feels comfortable to advance start to give a little lift of the front wheel just as you reach the lip. Aim to pop the front wheel over the edge and as it descends into the drop, committing your weight in and down to follow it smoothly. Although this move is with conviction it shouldn't be a huge lift of the front wheel; in terms of height we are not talking much at all. The distance the front is away from the ground will also be minimal;

just clearing the coping and then, as your weight is committed into the drop, the front wheel should be touching down on the ramp. Progress this until you feel confident to try the next step.

Nailing drop-ins requires some confidence in your bunny hopping technique. At the same point you began lifting the front. Now use this point to begin a bunny hop, this hop will be low and once again you must commit your weight fully into the descent. So as your front end goes over, so your weight will follow it and as you become comfortable with the rear hop your back wheel will start to clear the coping. This first stage will require patience and really use the online video to get a feel for the move. Once you have this first stage sorted the move onto a taller ramp is going to be simple and you'll progress much quicker than you think.

OK so the taller ramp is now in sight but before we leave the smaller ramp we have to make a major change to our approach and learn one more variation. Start to come in at the ramp from an acute angle rather than head on. This will mean your bunny-hop-in will now change in shape quite dramatically. The front will still pop up over the coping but now you will turn the front into the ramp as you do with the commitment of weight now slightly to the side of the ramp and your bunny hop of the rear wheel will now be more of a sideways drag into the ramp.

**Get confidence from your bunny hop – commit that front end into the curve !**

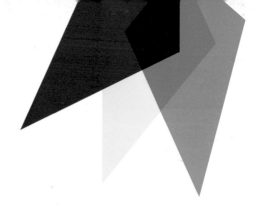

# X-UP

**Y**ou are nailing the basic riding with ease, you have great balance and most obstacles and ramps are within your reach. If you haven't started experimenting with tricks then I'd be surprised; there are so many different variations and moves to attempt, far too many for a book that has such a broad spectrum of skills to cover already. So I have chosen a selection of moves in this book that are the groundings for further experimentation. The very best riders are so advanced they fit two or three different moves into one jump.

**The X-up is an awesome jump and I'm starting with it because it's the first proper trail jump that I learned. It is also a very useable trick; some other moves require a certain take-off or distance, with an X-up though - if you can clear the jump then you X-up it.**

Approach the chosen practice jump (jump box or trail table-top is ideal) with the speed to clear the jump comfortably, and with descent height. Before you begin jumping stand over your bike, probably balanced against a wall or similar, do this with your knee pads on (which obviously you're wearing) and think about the space directly in front of you, the gap between your bars and legs. This is where you must fit the X-up in, so it's important to discover the difficulties you will experience. Now place your feet on the ground and spin the bars 180 degrees (in the direction away from your front foot) so that your arms cross over each over, and then stand back up on the pedals. To begin with this position will feel completely nuts. Getting used to it in this way will be very important, you almost need to get your body accustomed to stretching in this way; in the jump this position will be held for a very short time but your muscles, shoulders, wrists and hands need to move quickly and comfortably into and out of the position. Note while you balance like this how far back your legs are locked to give the move space, especially if you have pads on. Remember the movement of bars into this 180 position will require you to lock your knees back and out of the way. With that in mind your initial taster jumps should be about just trying that. Take-off with confidence and lock your knees back for a moment and think about the space you need. Remember to be quick with this though; locking your legs back for too long will create a stall and you could drift into an awkward landing position or crash.

Having thought about the space you need it's time to start 'X-ing' it up. The thing to remember is 'speed'. You need to move those

# "
# YOU NEED TO MOVE THOSE BARS AROUND SUPER QUICK
# "

bars around super quick and in a definite movement. First attempts will be just turning the bars small amounts to feel it. When you do this note how it affects the whole bike's position in the air. Keep messing with it and learning the sensation, once you're confident there's only one thing left to do... lock it round into a full X! I find that the only way to get it locked around is to concentrate on the hand pushing the bars (if you X left, away from a leading right-foot, then I'm talking about the left hand and vice versa). This pushing hand is what will get it locked out and is the focus. It will also be important to pull the bars back with determination to be recovered for landing. A quick movement at the top of the air-time axis is when to go for it. It will probably take quite a while to nail and you should expect some moments of bottling-out, totally natural and to be expected. The first committed attempt will bring the result you're after though, just think about moving it quickly and with conviction, lock it out and then return with the same snap.

**Lock your knees back and make way for the X**

# TAKING YOUR LIMBS OFF

**T**he natural progression for any rider who is enjoying their jump riding is to start removing their hands or feet. It is a very scary thing to do and it looks really cool – it's also the gateway to many other more technical tricks like Bar-spins and Tailwhips. I've always been a bit of a numpty at this stuff, in Trials riding there has never been much call for one-handers. So I've not really investigated the possibilities of this area of riding that much. I can manage simple one-handers or no-footers but much more than that I'd have to say I'm struggling. So for that reason the tuition side of this chapter is coming from guest 'instructor' Chris Smith, a rider famous for some crazy moves that involve removing hands and feet from there normal position on bars and pedals. I will happily read through Chris's explanation with you in the hope that I can finally get a bit of confidence in this area of riding. I've always thought it would be great to pull a perfect Can-can and perhaps now I will start to learn the secrets along with you.

Go online and visit www.mtbtricks.co.uk for videos and tutorials

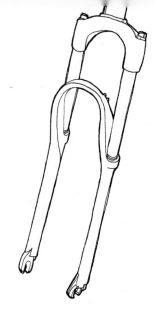

## Over to you Chris:

"The first time I saw a picture of BMX rider Ryan Nyquist doing a 'Suicide No-hander' I knew I had to have it in my trick bag, it just looked amazing. In the picture Ryan's bike was in a nose dive position with Ryan almost lying off the back with his arms impossibly outstretched behind him! It looked incredibly stylish and I spent the next few weeks on the case. I brought a big Jump style seat and raised my seat up so I could comfortably clamp it between my knees. I practised on the flat just gripping the seat with my knees and making the crucifix position. I then started sessioning the local jump-box, starting with perfecting one-handers first. I then started working on loosening my grip on both sides of the bar. The next step was to begin to remove my hands a few inches away, then progressing to clapping them behind my back. A few days later I had managed to nail them 'Nyquist style'. I found the more relaxed I got with the move the easier it got; these days I can hit a 40-foot step down at full speed and chuck a suicide in at any time. If I'm feeling brave I will even go for a suicide during a 360- but let's just keep to the basics for now!

Finding a safe jump will be key to the learning these tricks, so find a jump with a good run in and run out. It should be one you can jump every time with a fair bit of air-time, a jump box or a tabletop is ideal. Tricks are done at the 'peak' of your jump, so learning where this peak is vital. Think about the jump in three stages - take off and set up is stage one, stage two is the 'peak' where the bike is weightless and the final stage is the inevitable landing. Ideally all tricks should be completed during that second important stage, the 'peak' of your jump.

So let's start by taking your feet off. Approach the jump as you would normally but slightly faster and as the bike leaves the take off let the front end go light but be central on the bike. As the bike nears the peak jump both your feet from the pedals by doing a small splits style movement – jumping them out sideways, it's a small explosive snap of the feet at first. The move happens in milliseconds until you're happy doing it over bigger jumps. You can actually practise this move on the flat ground to get your confidence up. In the air keep your arms stiff and the bike locked in position. Have a quick glance at your pedals and replace your feet and land as normal.

"

# KEEP YOUR ARMS STIFF AND THE BIKE LOCKED IN POSITION

„

Removing your hands:
Taking your hands off mid air is a pretty impressive move again. The same three steps apply for this move so look for the 'peak' of the jump again. Practice one-handers and no-handers on the floor whilst riding along on flat ground. Getting you and your bike in the correct position is fairly important for learning this move. I found a key element for me was raising my seat so I could pinch the nose of the saddle with the insides of my knees.

**"**

## GETTING YOU AND YOUR BIKE IN THE CORRECT POSITION IS FAIRLY IMPORTANT FOR LEARNING THIS MOVE

**"**

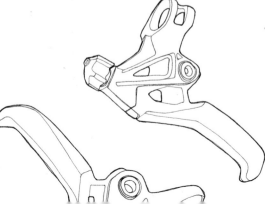

For the suicide no hander approach the jump a little faster than normal, as you take off aim to get the bike horizontal in the air at its peak. As the bike gets into this position pinch the nose of the saddle with your knees and simultaneously throw yourself back away from the bar and arch over backwards; the bike should level out as you extend your arms back. Keep your eyes on those handlebars and grab them quickly before the bike starts to descend into the landing.

Working your way up to this trick is crucial. That 'on the flat' practice will be very handy – at this time concentrate on the explosive movement. Once jumping start by loosening your grip on your bars then take it step by step working your way, jump by jump, further away from your bars. Good luck guys'n'gals!"

It's clear Chris thinks we should be taking this in 'dolly-steps' so don't go blasting off a ramp and just letting go. Start with concentrating on that feeling of the 'peak' of the jump. Your practice of the X-up will have given you a good understanding of this hopefully. It should be obvious when to start trying to 'let go'. If it isn't then perhaps you need to do a bit more practice. The graduation of loosening your grip or lifting the feet away should be tiny movements to begin. Don't rush these moves, every jump you get a little bit better – remember what Chris said "As he relaxed it got easier and easier".

**Find the peak – then explode the movement – be quick!**

"Looking back I could have never dreamt of a more perfect career in my wildest dreams - trust me, I have been dreaming a lot."

**Hans Rey**
World MTB Trials Champion, CEO of 'Wheels for Life' charity and Martyn Ashton's cycling hero since childhood

# TRIALS DEMON

Trials riding is such a technical sport but the foundations of all trials moves is balance and that means any practise of trials skills is a very useful thing for any bike rider. You have already learnt many of the basic skills needed to enjoy this section: ultimately the Trackstand is the most important but the wheelie and wheelie drop-off will have given you the confidence to progress. So don't think of this as a new section – just an extension of the good work you've already put in.

# GOING UP
## WALLS, STEPS AND LOGS

**T**his is a very useful move and as a trials rider I can't think of a more important skill to learn well and be confident with. Trials requires amazing bike control, but even if you don't want to concentrate on this area too much the basic skills will come in very handy on the XC trail. I've always found that it's this ability to get up an obstacle that has allowed me to take advantage of my Trials skills over non Trials riders when out riding XC. The level of obstacle you will encounter on an average XC trail is no more than 2ft high at the most so this level is well within the reach of everyone. The secret is to gain confidence in the technique on an obstacle that is simple and can be treated as our uniform practice spot.

**I find walls are the very best practice zones for this move so identify your wall for practice with these things in mind: a step up of no more than 30cm, plenty of riding space into the wall, and plenty of riding space on top of the wall. As Trials riding has developed over the years, many techniques have been mastered for ascending obstacles. In fact the record for riding a bike up a vertical wall now stands at something like 2ms, which is absolutely huge! Even at that extreme height the process of riding up an obstacle is still just a simple matter of following a few stages in the process... just way bigger than when you start out.**

There are many different techniques that Trials riders use for getting up obstacles, especially those ones that stand as high as 2ms! We don't need to get too fussy about all that though. You just need the confidence to negotiate an obstacle on the trail or begin a journey into trials riding that is positive. So we will concentrate on the most common and simple way to attack an obstacle.

Approach the wall at a slow pace with your weak foot forward, at about one bike's length away from the wall pedal through onto your leading foot beginning the lift of the front wheel with the bottom of your weak foot and getting full height to clear the top of the wall as your strong foot powers it. As the front wheel touches down on the wall you need to have reset your front foot to lead and then chop again on the pedal to create a burst of momentum to begin your lift of the back wheel up the wall. To get this lift efficient concentrate on your toes hooking over the pedals, pushing back and up to lift the rear wheel up the wall – just like you did earlier in the Bunny Hop.

At this height it will be quite easy to break the move down into three stages. Placing the front wheel on top is stage one. Resetting the pedal is stage two, followed by a last kick of your strong foot and back wheel lifting up is three. As your chosen obstacle gets bigger, these stages will need to become smoother in transition, and quicker. Eventually they will be one smooth process.

You may find that it's difficult to get that 'chop' of the pedal in. This will most likely be because you're carrying too much speed. Rather than slow down and ride at an uncomfortable pace – try completing the lift with just the 'rear wheel lift' action you learnt before. This is just as valid a move and will get much the same result. Remember there are no hard and fast rules to these things, experimentation will see you doing it your way, if you get up the wall/log/root then the job is done and that is all that matters.

*Place the front on top and then hop!*

## REMEMBER THERE ARE NO HARD AND FAST RULES TO THESE THINGS

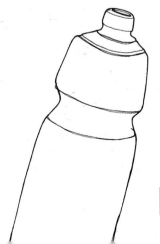

# CONTROL MOVE 1: SMALL FRONT HOPS

**T**his element is designed to take that track-standing skill to the next level and make the following Trials moves a reality. It's not exactly glamorous, I grant you. It would never dress the final run of an X-games gold medallist or be mentioned by a world class down hill racer in the post win interview. However small correctional hops (essentially what we are learning here) are a fundamental skill that will get you out of a tight spot. It isn't pretty but its function will allow you to get extreme confidence in your balance. The combination of small endos and front hops will create a see-sawing action that can turn you around on the spot! Out on the cross country trail this low speed trickery will prove invaluable. As a developing Trials rider this control will be the fundamental form of balance that you need whilst pursuing the vast array of more technical skills that Trials riders use.

Go online and visit
www.mtbtricks.co.uk
for videos and
tutorials

**I'm never going to inspire you with words like: useful, dependable and functional. These are the words that really tell the font-hops story, but like an honourable serviceman in battle the impressive and vital role will be lost when the Admiral tells his tale. However without 'Private Front-Hop' and 'Seaman Mini Endo' attacking furiously in the trenches the battle could never have been won. These unsung heroes will never impress your mates, but by the time they catch you up on the trail you will have forgotten what you wanted to tell them.**

Way back when I was riding motorcycle trials, before I had ever set my eyes on mountain biking in fact, I remember visiting a pre-season motorcycle show that changed my path in riding. These pre-season events were where the manufacturers displayed their new product; I was excited and looking forward to viewing all of the beautiful bikes on show. This would be the catalyst of many hours day-dreaming about the bikes I'd seen and how (if there was any justice) I would save enough pocket money to buy one. This particular show in question opened my eyes to Trials riding on bicycles. As a piece of entertainment the organiser had invited the UK's very best Biketrial rider, Stuart Matthews to come along and do a demonstration. I watched Stuart in amazement! I could not believe what he was doing on his bike. The really impressive part of his riding to me wasn't

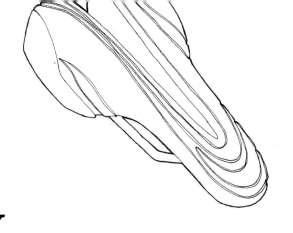

# " I COULD NOT BELIEVE IT AND WAS SUDDENLY VERY INTERESTED IN THIS SPORT

**"**

how high he could climb or how far he could leap. It was the fact that he could hold his balance indefinitely. It wasn't a matter of how long he could hold it, he simply did not need to place his feet down! His control of the Trackstand combined with mini endos and front-hops gave him absolute balance. At one point in the demonstration he made a small mistake and lost his balance whilst on top of some pallets. Instead of jumping clear of the bike - which is what I would have done - he hopped the bike sideways and dropped off the side of the pallets. Now moving sideways and falling he was sure to crash on landing but when his wheels touched down he continued to fight for balance. His upper body weight was off to one side but by hopping furiously with both back and mostly front wheels he finally got the bike back underneath him and in control. I could not believe it and was suddenly very interested in this sport that would take me on a whole new journey.

Learning these control hops is another great play-riding trick that can be perfected just riding around outside your house in the street. Start by getting into the trackstand position against a curb, just like you did when you learnt to Track Stand. With the brakes on, knees and arms slightly flexed you are going to pull back and up and at the same time straightening the bars to ride away. You will have just learnt to front hop. Make sure you learn this simple one hop strategy in both left and right directions before moving on to the next step.

Once you can easily perform a single hop with confidence it is just a matter of increasing the amount of hops away from the curb. This will be an enjoyable challenge that is similar to learning volleys with a football; it will take time but it won't be long before you can suddenly do double figures.

The real breakthrough will be the moment you are hopping the front wheel one way and lose your balance, instinct will take over and in an effort to get the bike back under you you'll perform a corrective hop back the other way. This is the moment when the real use of front-hops will click into place. It will most likely happen when you are hopping your least favourite direction and the corrective hop will

# "THIS SIMPLE PROCESS WILL DEVELOP COMPLETE CONTROL OF FRONT-HOPS"

feel natural. Just keep practising using a supportive curb because this will help concentrate your balance and keep your mind on the task in hand, instead of on track standing. Hop away from the curb in small hops your weight leading the way, each hop bringing the bike back underneath you. As balance moves either increase the hop to keep up or allow the corrective impulse and change of direction to happen with a hop back towards the curb. The aim is to hop out ninety degrees from the curb, using corrective hops is great but always try to regain control and get going back in the right direction. Once you have reached ninety degrees you can start to hop back to the curb. This simple process will develop complete control of front-hops in both left and right directions. When you can turn ninety degrees and then return all the way back to balancing against the curb again you will be a very controlled rider indeed.

*Let your weight lead the way. Mix it up with The Endo*

# CONTROL MOVE 2: THE ENDO

**T**he Endo is a really useful trick that will bring hours of fun and really develop your riding into a much more dynamic style. Endoing is the skill of using the front brake to lift the rear wheel off the ground and as you get better a new way of steering the bike around tight corners at low speed. At high speed this trick is a very cool way of stepping your back wheel out in a similar way to the Power Slide.

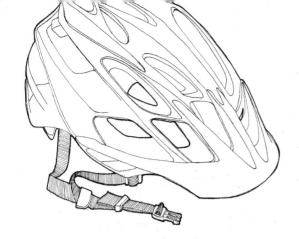

**I'm a particular fan of this move I must be honest; it totally fits into my 'play riding' mentality. I love riding around out the front of my house just messing about with simple tricks and endoing is a move to make any curb-side location fun.**

My fascination with this move began when I was a schoolboy Motorcycle trials rider back in the eighties. At that time 'trick riding'- as we called it – was just making its way into the moto version of Trials. This trick riding began with front wheel moves as simple as hopping the front wheel from side to side. The Endo came later but was one of the transforming skills that developed the sport at that time. It made a huge difference because suddenly the top riders could manoeuvre the bikes in very small spaces and create approach lines to obstacles that weren't previously possible without hopping skills. I had discovered the Endo through motorcycles but it had originated from Cyclo-trials riding; the sport we now recognise as Biketrials was developing in Spain at the time and talented moto riders had just started realising the advantages of the tricks that the sport of Cyclo-Trials used – the Endo being one.

I can't really over state how cool this move is once you have confidence with it. Imagine how dramatic a change it would be to your car if all of a sudden you could steer the rear wheels as well as you can the front. Every car park space would suddenly be way easier to get into wouldn't it. The Endo makes your bike a two-wheel-steering machine; that's how brilliant this move is.

The trick itself is a combination of hard front-wheel braking and the rider moving body weight forward to let the rear-wheel lift off the ground. With subtle changes in weight position and body movement it's possible to swing the back end of your

Go online and visit www.mtbtricks.co.uk for videos and tutorials

bike left or right. A normal curb stone is the perfect place to try this move, like I said the 'out front' playing on your bike element is great.

You should start learning by riding off the curb and applying the front brake with force to feel the reaction of the rear wheel lift. It goes without saying that you need to do this in a steady process of experimentation. We are doing it off a curb because this will automatically move your weight forward and over the front wheel. So these first few attempts need to be tame braking, a big fist full of front brake will only end in you going over the handle bars and knocking your teeth out (not good). So get used to the front brake and let the rear wheel lift up, if only a few centimetres. An important thing to note here: the front-brake is all controlling in this move, if you release it the rear-wheel will drop back down. Of course – like the wheelie – there is a point of no return but it's harder to reach than you think.

*START BY RIDING OFF THE CURB AND APPLYING THE FRONT BRAKE TO FEEL THE REACTION OF THE REAR WHEEL LIFT*

After you are used to this simple process of front brake action start to combine the other elements of the move in. Still off the curb start to compress your knees and then lift them up as you apply the front brake; this will dramatically increase the lift of the rear-wheel. As that rear comes up start to control it by letting your knees bend again so that the frame of the bike moves up and in towards your body. Because the bike is now compressed between your bent knees you have the ability to push it back down as you wish. A combination of pushing the rear wheel down and gentle release of the front brake will develop a smooth second-half to the move.

From this point it is just a matter of experimenting with the move. Keep using the kerb stone as a practice point because it will allow you to get results without having to force your weight over the bars aggressively to get a result, and there for is a safer way of practice. As your confidence grows you can start to move the rear wheel to the side. Practise this by rolling off your curb at an acute angle and just before you

apply the font brake steer slightly in towards the curb, a commitment of your weight out towards the road now will bring the rear-wheel up as normal but it will also swing out because you have moved weight that way; the bike will also pull to get the front wheel straight, so that turn at the start of the move will help create the turn but also ensure you end the move pointing in the right direction. Make sure you attempt this in both directions right from the outset. You will undoubtedly have a strong side but that can be fixed with practice. It will be far more beneficial if you can turn the bike both ways like this. Once you are comfortable with moving the back wheel down off the curb try mixing small front hops with small Endos - as explained in the previous chapter - these small control hops will create a great foundation for balance and control, especially when Trials riding.

Another great thing about this move - once you have a grasp on it - you can now just play with it and get comfortable using it on the trail. The more advanced versions of the move like the rolling endo are extreme but easily achievable. To start that process just find yourself a nice gentle grass slope and start committing weight over the front end and applying some force from the front-brake. It goes without saying that you should start gently and experiment. As long as you let the bike come up to you it will be controllable; front brake on, locked out legs and rear wheel high are not a good combination.

*Control the height with your knees - mix it up with control move 1*

# BACK HOPS

There is no other move that distinguishes you more as a Trials rider than Back-hops. It's a milestone in your Trials riding development because it's almost the qualification that proves you've got what it takes. There are many reasons why learning back-hops is important as a Trials rider, mainly it's one of the most useful manoeuvres a rider can obtain and use; it will make attempts at obstacles possible that otherwise were not. As well as being useful, back-hops are cool. There aren't many riders who wouldn't want to be able to sit their bike on the back wheel and put it anywhere he/she wants. Once you have them dialled, that's what back-hops enable you to do. The bike is standing on its end; your bike's wheel base is no longer the surface area that you must control, now only the rear wheel is touching the ground and you can turn the bike 360 degrees on that small point of contact – you have to be pretty good at back-hops to do that though. As a competition Trials rider you would need to focus on back-hops and get them as accurate and controlled as possible; particularly because many modern Trials moves stem from back-hops these days.

**My first exploits into Biketrials riding (meaning on pedal powered cycles not motorbikes) was on 20-inch wheeled competition bikes. In my first year of competing I learnt all the fundamental moves plus some of the very modern and new skills that were advancing the sport so rapidly – back-hops being one of them.**

It wasn't long before my cycling attention was drawn to mountain bike events and I was thinking about racing. At the very first mountain bike event I went to see (National level event) there happened to be a Trials contest for UK's best MTB racers to try in the evening. At this stage in my career I was the UK's top comp Trials rider on 20-inch but no one at this event new about that sport or me; it was a tiny developing niche. My friends I was at the event with egged me and another 20-inch rider to enter the evening comp and try Trials riding on mountain bikes. So I entered into the very positive and relaxed nature of this mountain bike event and tried my luck against the cream of the crop in mountain bike Trials. The atmosphere was awesome, with a decent sized crowd

# *EVERY MOVE YOU LEARN NOW IS GOING TO MAKE HUGE GAINS IN ABILITY*

following the competitors around a small course of obstacles. At 20-inch Biketrial events we weren't used to crowds, not even at our biggest events, it felt great having people watch and appreciate the efforts of all the competitors. I got to one particular section and looked at the designated route, all the riders before had failed because of the tight nature of the route and a nasty drop off of a stack of pallets. I knew exactly what to do though and rode in, back-hopped around the troublesome turn and off the pallets with ease, because I could back-hop no problem – in the tiny world of Biketrials you were a no-one if you couldn't. The assembled crowd gasped! They had never seen this technical level of Trials riding, and I was genuinely surprised by that. It turned out that important people in MTB had been watching and I was snapped up for sponsorship, I was featured in the UK's best MTB mag the next month, including a cover shot. My career path took a sharp change in direction that day, I had never planned it but I had showcased Trials riding skills to the top people in a sport who at that time had no knowledge these skills even existed. They did exist but weren't created by me; I was just in the right place at the right time. The simple Back Hop had just changed my life.

I can't promise that Back Hops will have quite such a dramatic change in your life as they did mine, but I can promise this skill will transform your riding ability drastically.

We are at the point in this book were the basics have been taught and now you have stepped on a steep learning curve. Every move you learn now is going to make huge gains in ability; the fundamental skill of back-hops points you to so many more riding opportunities that this point of the book has the steepest learning curve of all.

Go online and visit www.mtbtricks.co.uk for videos and tutorials

Back Hops

# "

# THE AIM IS NOW TO GET COMFORTABLE WITH THIS PROCESS

# "

We are going about the Back Hop learning process in much the same way as the previous techniques, we are breaking it down into very obvious stages so that you can understand why it works and then step by step build the technique you need. So our starting point is on a nice flat surface (short grass is ideal), plenty of space. Ride along slowly in the approach position, and in a very light gearing. Start practising lifting the front end as high as possible from one sharp hit on the front foot - making sure the height is deliberately stopped by tons of back-brake at the high point – then letting the wheel drop back down. It will take a while for you to gauge the speed for success at this, the gearing will feel very light and the slow speed needed for your pedal stroke to have effect will feel very slow; stick with it though, keep going until you can get that front end up close to the balance point and then force it back down with back-brake. It is important to note that you shouldn't be making a complete pedal stroke. This lift is

coming from a sharp, hard and determined crank of your strong foot, but the pedal stroke is not completed, rather you return the strong foot back so you are ready to go again. Pedal then brake, remember that.

The next stage is simple progression, you have honestly done the hard part, you can nearly Back Hop (not been much hopping yet though has there?). On your next attempt try and get anther stab at the pedal in before the front touches down; applying the rear brake at the peak of the move as before. To achieve this step it will require committing your weight to the back of the bike so concentrate on that, your seat is low, you're on short grass, you're not going fast and you are wearing a decent helmet... go for it! Pedal then brake, pedal then brake! Now practise this system of pedal-brake-pedal-brake pedal-brake. You are very close to gaining complete control of back-hops.

The last stage requires you to add the hop. So perform three pedal-brakes and

then on the last pedal stroke combine it with a slight compression of the knees and release that compression when you pedal, also pull up with your arms. Aim to jump the bike in the air from this and land with that rear-brake applied. The aim is now to get comfortable with this process and then start trying to land it and get another pedal-brake in before the front comes down. Initially this will feel really uncomfortable and difficult – mainly because it is really difficult – but don't be put off. Keep coming back to the basics and breaking it down into segments. If you find it frustrating and too hard; go back to the earlier stage and continue practising pedal-brake. Watch the podcast and let the move sink into your brain, and when you're doing it think about that image.

*Pedal then brake, then pedal then brake, then pedal then...*

# TRIALS DROP-OFF AND BACK-HOP CONTROL

**I**f your progression has gone well then you've learnt back-hops and will now be thinking about how to put them to good use. The uses for back-hopping are diverse; as I mentioned before, an elite competition Trials rider can perform nearly every other Trials move from a static back-hopping position. The Trials drop-off is really the most infamous skill Trials can offer though; to any rider who can't back-hop watching a Trials rider negotiate seemingly impossible drops from high ledges is an awesome sight. The thing is as soon as you have good back-hop control the only difference between a 3ft drop and a 3m drop is in the mind. The important bit at the edge is all about back wheel control and confidence. Of course I'm not recommending you start hopping off 3m drops. Drops from these heights require tons of practice, but once you have control and start riding off some ledges you'll be surprised how achievable a big drop will feel. How high you go is up to you, but don't go setting any goals just yet; at this stage we need to get the important control sorted then you are free to start a career of trials base jumping if you wish.

I have spent many years riding MTBs in magazines and over that time I have built strong friendships with a couple of photographers that I work with. One of those is the famous MBUK snapper, Steve Behr. Back in the nineties Steve used to organise photo trips where he would get a group of pro-riders together (8 or 9 riders usually) and take us away to a great sunny location. We would spend a week or so finding great features for the magazine. Steve always had a rough (literally) idea of what he wanted to shoot; usually written on a scruffy piece of paper that he'd scribble on whilst on the phone discussing possible stories with the editor. The list always took a similar format; usually a roster of the riders names on the trip, then a few ideas of things they could do for interesting stories. Over the years on these trips I had grown some what of a reputation landing some big trials moves that always shot well. So after a few trips my name was usually followed by the words – something big!

# "

## *POINTING STRAIGHT AT A HUGE ROCK FACE THAT DROPPED DOWN TO THE BEACH "I'M GONNA RIDE OFF THAT!"*

"

You're probably wondering what the hell this has to do with drop-off control; bear with me, it's actually a good example of my lack of it.

On one particular trip I couldn't come up with anything, I kept looking for gaps to jump or walls to ride but nothing turned up that ticked the box of 'something big'. In the end I was forced to take emergency action. We had reached the last day of shooting and I was desperate. Steve found me down by the sea front – still searching – and asked if I had anything. I didn't want to loose my reputation (stupidly I'd grown quite proud of it) so when Steve asked if I had anything, I blurted out "yes, that!" pointing straight at a huge rock face that dropped down to the beach "I'm gonna ride off that!"

Go online and visit www.mtbtricks.co.uk for videos and tutorials

The drop in question was later measured at 16ft! Well over my comfort zone in terms of drop-offs, by about 2ms. The ledge from which I dropped was a little bumpy (and here's the lesson) so I decided I wouldn't fanny around on the precipice, rather I would make one definite hop to the edge and then send it (me) off the edge with gusto. Basically I knew if I spent any amount of time controlling the bike at the ledge I would see sense and bottle out – but that was out of the question now, Steve had his camera set up and all my friends were watching. You can guess that it didn't go well; I did the drop, with no control and smashed my teeth on my

"

## YOUR FIRST TASK IN MAKING PROGRESS TO BIG DROPS IS VERY SIMPLE; PRACTICE LOADS

"

seat when I landed, over 5 metres straight down from where I began. I spent two weeks afterwards with strained ligaments in my forearms, I couldn't close my grip or hold anything! Not my finest moment and certainly not a great example of control, but that's exactly my point. The height of drops you attempt are not important, clearly any old Muppet can do a big drop. Having the control at the edge is what is important; if you can't hold your nerve at the edge of a drop, chances are it's too big for you at that stage, because the bigger the drop, the more confidence and control you will need to leave that ledge in the right shape to survive. Let's get that control shall we?

The notable difference between back-hopping and controlled back-hopping comes down to 'directional adjustment'. In short: being able to hop forward in the pedal-brake-pedal-brake way I taught earlier is a cool trick but off a drop it wouldn't serve you well. So your first task in making progress to big drops is very simple; practise loads. No secret I'm afraid, just keep back hopping, but here are some tips that will develop the control needed for drops: once you can happily hop along the flat on your rear wheel (which should be celebrated) aim to get the hops as small as you can. Once you've got the hops going really small; try and hold the bike on the spot for a moment before setting off again. Many people learn to hop on the back wheel by holding a fist full of rear-brake and pulling back, constantly hopping the bike backwards to stay on the rear wheel. Of course this is useless because no one in their right mind goes off drops backwards. So this is why I had you learn hops in the way I did; you can go forwards, but this practice is all about slowing it down and being so confident in your control that you can stop the bike, hold it there and even turn left or right a little bit.

## "START SMALL WITH DROPS; EVEN USE A CURB AT FIRST TO REHEARSE THE CONTROL AT THE TOP "

Don't put the following into action until you can comfortably control your back-hops; it is just practice so enjoy it and think about how far you've come.

Start small with drops; even use a curb at first to rehearse the control at the top. Unfortunately though, a curb drop isn't going to let you experience the sensation of dropping so try and find a wall that has plenty of space at the top for manoeuvre and a drop of no more than wheel height. At this height you can get away with most errors but you also have enough time to force the rear down in front of you to smooth out the drop.

Hop to the ledge and as the back wheel reaches the precipice make tiny adjustments until you are happy – then commit to the drop. It's important that you remember not to go back on this decision. Once you commit then this drop is happening. The commitment is unlike the drop into a ramp though; don't move your weight forward, rather let the front drop out over the ledge, lowering to a point where your weight is right back, front pedal loaded. The front wheel is so low it's

now almost horizontal. With a sharp and definite kick on the pedal force the bike rear wheel down and fast. Try and notice that your front wheel has only dropped a small amount before the rear wheel touched down. The back end travelled the distance down but your bike almost did it in two stages; lowering of the front, then a sharp movement forcing the back down to a locked rear wheel on landing.

As drops get bigger this lowering of the front gets ever more important; this is where you need to be aware of the confidence! If you can't control the bike at the edge for fear of the drop... it's too big. The technique happens at the ledge, it's at that point you create a chance of a successful result.

Compression of your knees at the landing will become more important as you get higher but that is natural progression, and should be obvious. Watch the podcasts and let the feeling sink in, make sure you understand the control and confidence needed.

**Drop that front wheel low and then force that back wheel down for a steep landing**

# ROCK WALK
## AND ROCK
## WALK DROP

**T**he rock walk is a progression of the Endo and front wheel lift you learnt earlier, and in learning this you can gain even more control of your bike. The eventual aim of the trick is to be able to flip-flop along, endoing the front wheel 180 degrees then landing it to swing the front wheel around 180 degrees and thus rock-walk along. Realistically I can't justify this move as a viable form of travel... it will take a while to get down the shops like it. The rock-walk is more about advancing the limits of your bike handling and nailing a trick that looks pretty cool. The rock-walk is also the basis for a drop-off move that is one of my favourite tricks of all time; the rock-walk 360 drop. This move looks really technical and scary but it's actually really easy to learn once you have the rock-walk perfected.

This is also a great time for me to pay homage to a rider that inspired me to ride mountain bikes (and many, many others); Mr Hans 'no way' Rey. Hans was the very first Trials rider to use mountain bikes for Trials riding, and his promotion of mountain biking through his trials demos around the world is one of the big reasons the entire sport took off like it did in the nineties. Hans Rey, although an exponent of the most niche of mountain biking disciplines (Trials) is one of the most famous names in the sport. The tricks he used to excite mainstream audiences were all derived from BMX and Trials and the Rock-Walk was one of the classic moves Hans used back in the day. That doesn't mean the move is outdated, the way Hans used it probably is but like I said, learning this move is about advancing your skills.

I first saw Hans riding at an International Trials competition in Spain, it was 1992. Hans was already a star of mountain-biking which I was a few months away from discovering and he rode for the infamous Team GT which had all the great racers of the time on board. My first vision of Hans was at the bike check in area. This area was where competitors entered their bikes for the following day's competition and an expectant crowd had gathered to watch the top competitors bring their bikes in. I'd liken it to a boxing fight weigh-in, there was a great atmosphere.

Hans arrived onto the platform; he just rolled up on and handed his bike over to be checked. It passed of course but that's when Hans the showman took over, he quickly hopped onto his gleaming GT Zaskar and first did a complete circle of back-hops, then promptly exited the stage pulling perfect rock-walk hops and out of sight. The crowd went nuts and Hans had just assured himself a good supportive following for the following day's comp. I was left struck by the control the guy had displayed on his bike, the Rock-Walk seemed impossible to explain physically, but when Hans had done it I was amazed at how easy it looked, so smooth and so controlled; it seemed like a good way to travel (it isn't). It had captured my imagination and Hans Rey had just hooked another rider into the exciting World of mountain bikes.

## "
## THE ROCK-WALK IS ONE OF THE CLASSIC MOVES, THAT DOESN'T MEAN IT'S OUTDATED, THIS MOVE IS ABOUT ADVANCING YOUR SKILLS
## "

# MAIN AIM OF LEARNING THIS ROCK-WALK IS TO ADVANCE YOUR HANDLING

The beginning of the Rock-Walk is the endo, which you learnt already so I won't go into much more detail here; only to say that to get a 180 degree Endo you will need to turn into it hard. If your favourite way to Endo is swinging to the right then you will turn in left hitting the front-brake just before your bars make 90 degrees. The momentum and weight committed will bring your rear-wheel around in the air and practice will see this distance develop into a 180 degree move. This process will take some time, but remember that the main aim of learning this Rock-Walk is to advance your handling. If you get this far you're half way to a Rock-Walk but you also just perfected Endos to the left.

Back to the Rock-Walk: the front end is spun 180 degrees by landing the rear-wheel with a locked rear-brake. Use the combination of your momentum and gripped rear-tyre to swing the front wheel

around to your left. To create the spin think about looking hard over your shoulder to the direction you wish to go; this will pull your shoulders around and create the twist you need to spin. Remember it's your weight and momentum that lead this trick. One Endo combined with one front wheel lift should spin you through 360 degrees. To have the trick pegged you need to be able to follow on from this straight into another set.

The Rock-Walk drop I mentioned is the ultimate use for the move and should be attempted off very small drops to begin. The Endo element starts right on the ledge and you must wait for the right moment to spin the front end off into the drop. The only difference in this move is that when you commit to spinning the front you also add a hop of the front wheel to pull it clear of the edge. If you start sensible (as with any trick) and progress with very small drops to begin, you really can convert the skill into a cool trick drop-off.

**Commit to a big endo then follow smoothly with the front-end spin: repeat!**

# SIDE
# HOPS:
# UP AND
# DOWN

**I** remember the first time I saw a rider side-hop up and over an obstacle; it was genuinely one of the first times anyone had used the technique – the rider performing it was the incredible Spanish legend Ot Pi. The obstacle in question was a skip and Ot used the move to escape by simply jumping out and over the side of this metal container. I'd never seen anything like it and couldn't believe it was possible. Looking at the technique you could well be thinking the same thing – 'how the hell do you do that?' – don't stress about it, this is a difficult technique but once the basics are dialled then progression is very quick.

Go online and visit www.mtbtricks.co.uk for videos and tutorials

**One major factor in getting this move in your trick bag will be making sure the supporting move – the Trackstand – is absolutely sorted. If your balance isn't an effortless process yet then give that a good session to begin. The reason being: side-hops up will require focus on the technique and achieving consistency without great balance will be more difficult. Also the art of side-hopping down an obstacle will need very good balance because the move takes place very close to the edge of the drop; you don't want to go off that drop before you intended so again the focus will be on balance. It's heartening to think that grasping such a technical move like side-hops is within reach, just by giving a bit more time to your Trackstand. It will make a world of difference.**

I use side-hops in my bike shows all the time. It gets such an amazing response from audiences because they can't believe the height possible. For a long time I held the World record for this move which I set on the famous TV show Record Breakers. That day was very nerve racking indeed – I'd practised side hops over the bar for hours on end the week before. Entering the studio, I was very confident I could clear the height of 43 inches (1metre 10cm) but the moment I saw the audience I was very nervous. Suddenly all the practice seemed out of context. I had practised in such a relaxed atmosphere, with plenty of time, and now I was in front of 400 people and the time schedule was completely set. The nerves built whilst I sat in my dressing room awaiting my call, I just kept telling myself to relax and concentrate on the basics of the move. By the time my call came to film I was in a far more relaxed mood; in fact I had decided to enjoy the crowd and give them a show. Under the rules I had three attempts at the record so my first go would be a 'feeler', I'd knock

> ## I USE SIDE-HOPS IN MY BIKE SHOWS ALL THE TIME. IT GETS SUCH AN AMAZING RESPONSE

the bar down but give it plenty of energy and the crowd a show. The second attempt would be the one and I'd make sure of it. All went perfectly to plan until my second attempt; I'd cleared the warm-up jumps easily and the first 'feeler' at the record had...felt, well it had felt very good. On the proper attempt I lined up alongside the bar and instead of concentrating on my technique I started thinking about the result and celebrating, the crowd cheering because the tension I'd created was pretty intense, but I was very confident I could do the height, I'd practised and practised... then I lost my balance! I panicked and jumped at the bar in a rush of hashed technique and energy. I hit the bar hard knocking it flying, and knew I'd just piled an awful lot of pressure on my shoulders. I had one attempt left. The crowd were on the edges of their seats, I was annoyed. I could have got this thing done in one attempt but I'd let myself off, now I'd missed the opportunity to nail it and the pressure was really on.

My only hope was to go back–to-basics and make sure I gave myself a chance. The mistake on the second attempt was because my mind had been off the simple task of balancing. This time I moved up alongside the bar and felt control come over me, I knew I was thinking about the right things now and I was determined not to mess this up. The crowd were silent and I concentrated hard on simply settling myself down and waiting for the right moment to unleash the energy needed. I remember that moment so clearly because it really was a perfect feeling of balance, the energy of the situation, the crowd creating an electric atmosphere, the studio lights and all eyes on me – it all just clicked into place and I had no doubt about the outcome. I cleared the bar with height to spare and now held a World Record.

Let's start with going up onto an object first. Look at the obstacle I'm using and try to find something similar, an obstacle that isn't too big and has plenty of room on top so you can make a mistake with no huge consequence. You will find – most probably – that your leading foot will dictate the direction that suits you, most riders feel comfortable going away from their lead foot (right foot forward, side hop left). So line up next to the wall and just balance and relax. The process of side-hopping up needs to be a smooth but very energetic movement. So think of all the next instruction as one smooth system.

Straighten the bars and compress your knees downwards letting your arms pull straight, taking the strain. As you compress start to look to the side, towards the point you want to land. Press down hard on your front foot and lift with the front wheel as the power comes in; your legs should be straightening, your arms bending under the pull upwards. Let the front wheel lead you up, and lean into the chosen direction.

Land the front wheel on top of the obstacle with a locked front-brake, then commit your weight onto it like when endoing. This will allow you to bring the rear-end up and over onto the obstacle. Ride away smiling!

It sounds very complicated but the way to approach this, to make it achievable, is you need to want it. If you think this move looks cool and useful, the desire will be there and watching the podcast will work, watch the slow-mo action and let the process sink into your thoughts. Success will require a smooth system of movement so keep that in mind, literally.

Side hopping down an obstacle happens in the reverse motion of up. So you don't need to pedal to create the movement, it should be a definite static bunny hop, committing your weight into the drop. The secret is forcing the rear-wheel down the drop to take the sting out of the landing, really straighten your legs and push the

rear-wheel down ahead of you. Land with the rear brake locked. The most important part of this move to remember is a definite move off the top and forcing that rear wheel down.

*Go away from your weak foot – load up that spring*

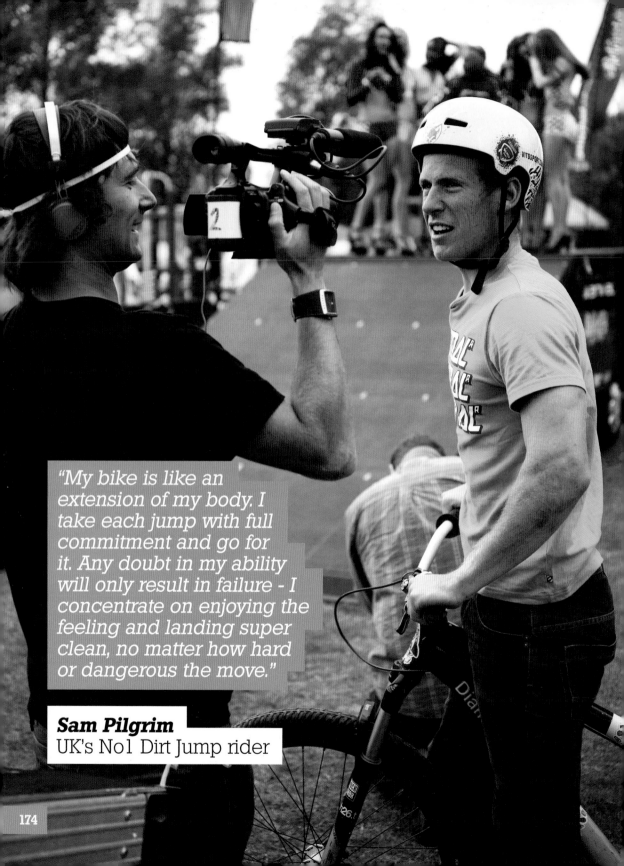

"My bike is like an extension of my body. I take each jump with full commitment and go for it. Any doubt in my ability will only result in failure - I concentrate on enjoying the feeling and landing super clean, no matter how hard or dangerous the move."

**Sam Pilgrim**
UK's No1 Dirt Jump rider

174

# FREE RIDING GENIUS

**F**ree-riding isn't just about going fast, riding over obstacles or pulling tricks. It's more a combination of all riding genres/techniques and it's exactly what it says on the tin; free... free from any rules or regulations. As a free-rider the course, trail, street or park put before you is completely open to interpretation. This element of mountain-biking is what has enabled the sport to adapt in so many ways and grow into the multi discipline, multi technology based sport it is today. I consider myself a free-rider; because I can handle most terrain but I wouldn't be recognised as a traditional free-rider like Chris Smith for instance, his form of riding is big suspension drops and jumps with BMX tricks added in. Mine is more of a technical balance and control based riding influenced by my Trials background. The point I'm making is there are no set rules, if you like a certain obstacle or venue for riding, then go with it, mix things up and do what feels good.

So in this section read with an open mind and don't necessarily concentrate on finding obstacles the same as the ones pictured. Rather think about the move itself and how it could be utilised for the riding where you are. This is really a message for the entire book; you don't have to have the same elements as those I've shown you. The beauty of mountain-bikes is they're adaptable in their basic form and can take on any riding terrain. Once you have identified the type of riding that suits you, a style of mountain bike will exist that has geometry and components to suit that style of riding.

# THE MANUAL

**T**he Manual is a diverse technique that will not only make you faster, more productive, safer and cooler, but will also create depth to lots of other moves because it can be linked with many to increase difficulty.

The art of Manual-ing is a controlled and sustainable wheelie – without pedalling. It sounds in the first instance like a show boating move that will serve little to enhance your riding, and there's nothing wrong with learning it just for that reason; nothing at all wrong with showing off and the Manual does look bloody good. However once you understand the Manual, and all its uses, it will be very hard to ignore it as an essential technique.

# " I LOVE WATCHING RIDERS USE THE MANUAL AS A CONNECTING TRICK "

Instances of where you'll use this move: in skate-parks where it will help you to interpret the ramp-decks (platforms on the tops of the ramps) in a smooth and fast manner. At the local BMX track or downhill trail it will provide a way of pumping speed through small doubles or whoops; you'll go through faster and with safety. Outside your house; as soon as you start learning this move there will never be another day where you can't think of anything to do 'out the front' on your bike. It will start by trying to perfect it then the endless game of 'how far' will come in, and that never ends.

I love watching riders use the manual as a connecting trick between two others. Our guest writer, Chris Smith is a great exponent of this. Chris will land a jump like a bar spin 'to manual', which means his front doesn't touch down on landing, rather he lands with his weight right back over the rear wheel and sustains the balance point by manualling. He will hold it until he reaches the drop or jump that's approaching and go into another move right out of the manual. Chris has them so dialled that

Go online and visit www.mtbtricks.co.uk for videos and tutorials

there probably aren't many of his tricks he can't do a Manual 'out-of' or 'in to'.

BMX racers manual through whoops on BMX tracks with such force and timing that it's actually a way of increasing speed through these tricky obstacles. I remember watching Frenchman and mountain bike racing legend, Cedric Gracia at a 4X World Cup race one time; he had gotten a bad start and followed the other three riders down the first half of the course at least a couple of bikes lengths behind – until the whoops came into play. The section of whoops on this course in Slovenia were very long and most riders treated them like two jumps; taking off from the first, landing in the down-slope of the fourth whoop and immediately jumping out of the fifth to clear the rest of the whoops, landing on the down-slope of the seventh whoop. It was then just a straight sprint to the finish. Cedric was behind but he could see the other riders lining up for these jumps and saw a gap. Choosing to sprint as fast as I think is possible at the whoops, you'd think when he reached the whoops Cedric's body weight will have been bucked to and fro. However as his front wheel took off from the lip of the first whoop Cedric held all his weight back over the rear wheel and then sucked up all the remaining whoops by holding the manual and letting his bent legs compress and extend as his rear wheel rode through the whoops. His top half was an accelerating picture of poise! His bike and legs moved frantically to work with the whoops; each pump over the whoops created more speed and Cedric passed two riders in the whoops. He exited the whoops so fast the other rider was passed in the sprint. It was very memorable win for my Volvo-Cannondale team mate at the time and a demonstration of how the manual can be vital to a racer.

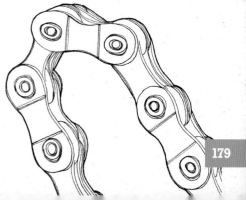

I wouldn't recommend hitting a set of whoops, flat out like Gracia just yet. The best way to learn Manuals is to perfect them on the flat – but I have devised a clever way of getting started which will speed the process up a bit, you'll be racing through the whoops in no time.

Because the most common way to enter a Manual is from a ramp, whoop or some other element in the terrain that aids to lift the front wheel, try this. Place a couple of planks on the ground, just under a bike's length apart. Start by approaching at a medium pace. To begin you just want to let the front wheel hit the first plank, and use that hit to initiate a lift and weight transfer to the rear – your aim is to clear the gap and land the front on the back-side edge of the second plank. You will probably find that as the rear wheel hits the first plank that the front wheel is forced down, and so landing on the second plank. That is totally normal and a good indication of how much weight needs to be committed to the rear. Keep practising until you can sustain the lift and suck up the hit of the rear tyre on the first plank, reaching the second with your front wheel. This movement of sucking-up the hit is done by letting your knees cushion the hit – as the bike come up, your knees bend and keep your body weight back and controlled.

Now increase the gap by double. The second plank will look a long way away now but don't think about the distance or speed, this is where the planks will help you. Same as before begin by hitting the first, weight back and sucking up the hit of the rear tyre with your knees. As the rear wheel drops off the first plank, push your knees straight back out towards being straight and you will feel the bike accelerate down the drop (even if it's only a very thin plank) and the front wheel gain height from that acceleration. Now you just hold that weight back with strong arms, balancing the height of your front wheel with your weight commitment to the rear – stop yourself going too high with tiny hits of the rear-brake. You will find that tons of rear-brake will slow you down loads and the momentum will be lost, so keep it minimal. Once you can get your front to the second plank start concentrating on getting the rear to the second plank and doing the same process again. Learning to get momentum out of such a small obstacle will demonstrate just how little you need to make this work.

Watch the video and get the feel for it, once you have it working the opportunities for Manuals will be everywhere and now you know how to practice them there is no excuse not to get them dialled.

**Flex those knees and keep your bum low man!**

# THE FAKIE

**T**he art of rolling backwards – or coming out of a move backwards is what Fakie is all about. I honestly can't think of many ways to argue this is a useful cross-country technique but bare with me here. Riding Fakie may not be a productive route down your local trail but it is one very impressive trick and in learning it you will undoubtedly learn greatly improved balance – your Trackstand especially will benefit especially.

It will improve your riding but the Fakie is essentially a really cool trick that you can put into action whilst riding street or skate parks. The simplest of obstacles can be made all the more exciting by adding this move into the mix. Take a slope for instance. Just rolling to a stop on that slope, then letting gravity do the rest and start rolling you back down it 'Fakie' is simple but very cool.

**As a Trials rider I use Fakie all the time because I'm constantly lining my bike up for obstacles – nothing gives you more options when faced with an obstacle than be able to roll the bike backwards away from the obstacle in question, and get the optimum amount of run-up.**

Like most tricks the Fakie originates from BMX but can be traced back to skate boarding before that. I've seen it used in some crazy places over the years; one of the best examples include dropping into a Vert ramp Fakie – not one for the faint hearted and something I admit I'd never dream of doing. The rider in question, Steve Geal used to be BMX Vert World Champion so I guess that's fair enough. I go 'all funny' just thinking about riding into a Vert ramp Fakie, it's a crazy idea. No matter how crazy an idea you think of though – chances are if you can think it up – somebody has probably tried to do it.

Whilst on a trip in Australia I remember seeing the Fakie put to the most incredible use ever. I was riding street with a group of local riders who were showing me around Cairns where I was staying for a week whilst doing a tour of demonstrations around Oz. The town itself was really cool, loads of lines to try everywhere. I wasn't too clued up on the local scene but had an idea there were a few good riders about, one particular guy really stood out amongst his mates, he was awesome. At this point I have to admit to never actually getting this kid's name, I was introduced

to him at the start of the evening but arrogantly I had let it go in one ear and out the other as I met about twenty riders that night. If I'd known he would impress me so much and years later I would be putting him in this book – well I'd have written it down. That evening this young dude who was riding a brakeless BMX was hammering around at full pelt at every spot we got to. Because he had no brakes he couldn't try many of the things myself and the other local riders were doing, we were all on Trials bikes and the brakes and low speed didn't suit this guy's bike at all - until we reached a sculpture in the town centre that was a riding dream. This huge piece of concrete was like a giant piece of ribbon and the curb around it was sloped like a small ramp. The locals all loved me riding this obstacle because to this point nobody had tried it, the jump up from the surrounding curb was about four feet high and it took me four or five goes before I

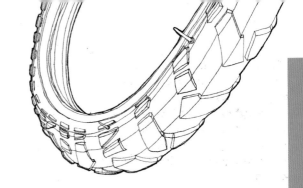

made it up onto this strip of undulating piece of rock, it was only about three feet wide. After about two minutes of playing the brakeless kid starts looking at the curb and then has a go, nailing it first time at hi-speed. His mates were suitably impressed as was I. Then to my surprise he rode in at speed and hit the curb, but jumped up 180 degrees and landed rolling backwards along the narrow strip, pedalling backwards furiously he controlled the Fakie and as he reached the other end of the concrete strip he committed his weight over the back and 180ed back off and down to terra firma so smoothly I couldn't believe it. Everyone went crazy and as we all congratulated him one of the locals explained that he's always pulling crazy moves like this. I asked the brakeless kid: "Man what made you think you could 180 up and then Fakie along that thing?" his answer was a smiling classic: "because I can't do 360's!"

## The Fakie

The process of learning a Fakie is best placed on something like a gentle grass slope. Your riding gear should be a light one but not too high because when pedalling backwards you need to stay ahead of the chain drive, so spinning the pedals slightly quicker than the bike is moving. The video is going to be very important for this move because some of the actions are very subtle; also it can look a little bit like you are pedalling the bike backwards – especially when done smoothly because the pedalling is so in time with the speed you are rolling. On the video you will be able to see that at times I've accelerated my back pedalling to demonstrate that it is necessary but isn't contributing to the roll.

So approach the slope and let the bike come to a stop. If you want you can go into a Trackstand before you start the Fakie, it will give you more time but it isn't necessary. To stop apply the front

## "

# THROUGHOUT THE FAKIE PROCESS, TRY NOT TO USE REAR-BRAKE BECAUSE IT WILL MAKE CONTROL REALLY HARD

## "

brake fully and lean forward as the brake locks, then backwards as you return your weight and release the brake. Throughout the Fakie process, try not to use rear-brake because it will make control really difficult. The front brake is your friend and the back-pedalling will also help you control the speed.

So as you pull back and start to roll backwards you will feel the front pedal push up into your foot as it tries to go backwards. Keep the pressure on that pedal and start to let the bike rock backwards and forwards on that balance point. Your pedal has become the brake on this gentle slope, get used to this sensation – once confident with holding this rocking Trackstand you should probably take five minutes to have a Coke and a smile to congratulate yourself on improving your Trackstand no end.

Go online and visit www.mtbtricks.co.uk for videos and tutorials

The Fakie

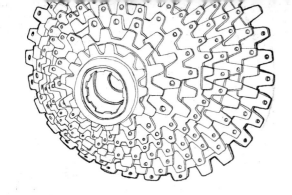

> ## "YOU NEED TO BECOME FAMILIAR WITH STEERING AND BALANCING THE BIKE BACKWARDS "

To progress the Fakie you need to let your weight on the pedal control the speed and then back-pedal onto your other foot, again catching the weight on the pedal. Then again back-pedal to catch the weight on your front foot again. It will feel difficult to do on your back foot so try and make that 'catch' a quick one, rescuing your balance on the front foot each time. Practice a bit then take it to a flat surface to improve.

The flat surface (pavement, skate park, car park etc) will mean you need to really put effort into the pull at the top of the move. Importantly you will need to keep the 'catch' of your balance with the pedals to a minimum because it will stop you quickly.

To get any real distance you need to become familiar with steering and balancing the bike backwards. I find that the steering works with my pedalling – so as I pedal my right foot back, my bars are turned to my left – then as I come round onto my left pedal my bars turn towards my right. This gives you space to pedal and combined in an equal pattern it will keep you going backwards in a straight line.

*For more momentum commit your head weight over the bars*

# FREERIDE ROLLING DROP-OFFS:

**H**ow high is too high? The pursuit of an answer to that question is never going to end in a nice way! Let's leave that quest to the riders who would find picking up a book a new experience - if you get what I mean. The technology of modern bikes is incredible and they can now happily handle drops way beyond the capability of most riders, and with the right guy onboard, they can happily soak up ridiculous heights that 10 years ago would not have been possible. The odd (literally) rider will push that limit too far but that isn't my focus for this chapter. This technique is simple and is as much about learning the physical requirements of the terrain needed for a successful freeride drop as it is about the technique of riding off the edge. This is true of many techniques – hardly anybody would attempt a jump without a take-off, because it isn't possible to get the height/distance needed. With freeride drops, a ledge is not the only requirement, you need somewhere to land.

One of the iconic events of modern 'Free-ride' mountain biking is that of the Red Bull Rampage. This event, held in Utah, USA, is all about riding down a mountain, like downhill racing – but there is no defined track and it's about getting to the bottom by using the craziest line possible, not so much like downhill racing!

Every year someone (usually a few) riders get really banged up from trying crazy lines that just don't seem possible, and sometimes they aren't possible. The majority of riders get down the course however, using ridiculous drops and jumps across chasms and it makes for a real cycling spectacle. From the beginning of this style of event the 'money shot' was who could do the biggest drop. One guy named Josh Bender got pretty famous from trying to go bigger than anyone else, and found the limit at 80ft or some crazy height? The trend for 'Hucking' off the biggest ledge has become less important at events like Rampage with judges scoring the more spectacular and technical rather than obvious 'throw your brain out' moves.

## YOU HAVE TO LEARN WHAT THE TERRAIN HAS TO OFFER, AND USE THAT

The rider's knowledge of the physics of riding has developed along with the bike technology. The drops attempted are still massive but they are landed far more regularly because the riders have identified what is needed to complete a successful drop – it isn't just a case of height.

Chris Smith is one of the UK's most prolific Free Riders and I remember seeing him ride his local quarry one time whilst on a photo shoot. Chris showed me a line off a ledge that then dropped at least 30ft down to a small sloping landing. I was nervous as he approached it and couldn't imagine doing the line myself. Even more amazing to me was when Chris, after his first successful landing, went back up and did the drop about another ten times for the photographer! Chris's consistency at dropping this height demonstrated how the techniques had developed. This drop had been 'built' by Chris and had all the elements needed for success. The bike had loads of suspension travel, Chris has bundles of talent and guts but also, and most importantly, the knowledge that bike + guts doesn't = success. You have to learn what the terrain has to offer, and use that.

**Knowledge is power – make good judgements on what is possible and what's not**

# THE WALL RIDE

There are walls everywhere and you can ride up them! I'm afraid, as you probably guessed, isn't true. As cool as it would be to ride 'Spiderman style' up a building; it's just not on I'm afraid. The problem that Spidey has managed to conquer with his CGI wall-walking is gravity. I wish there was a book like this that taught how to defy gravity, I'd buy it, but there isn't. Gravity sets a real boundary for us non-super heroes which means we have to look at a vertical wall in a different way.

So defying gravity is out and we lack the advantage of tiny hairs protruding from our tyres to help grip any surface – which is apparently how spiders do it (hairs on their feet not tyres). All is not lost however, because we can generate something that can help. You won't be able to defy gravity – but with momentum - you will be able to trick it.

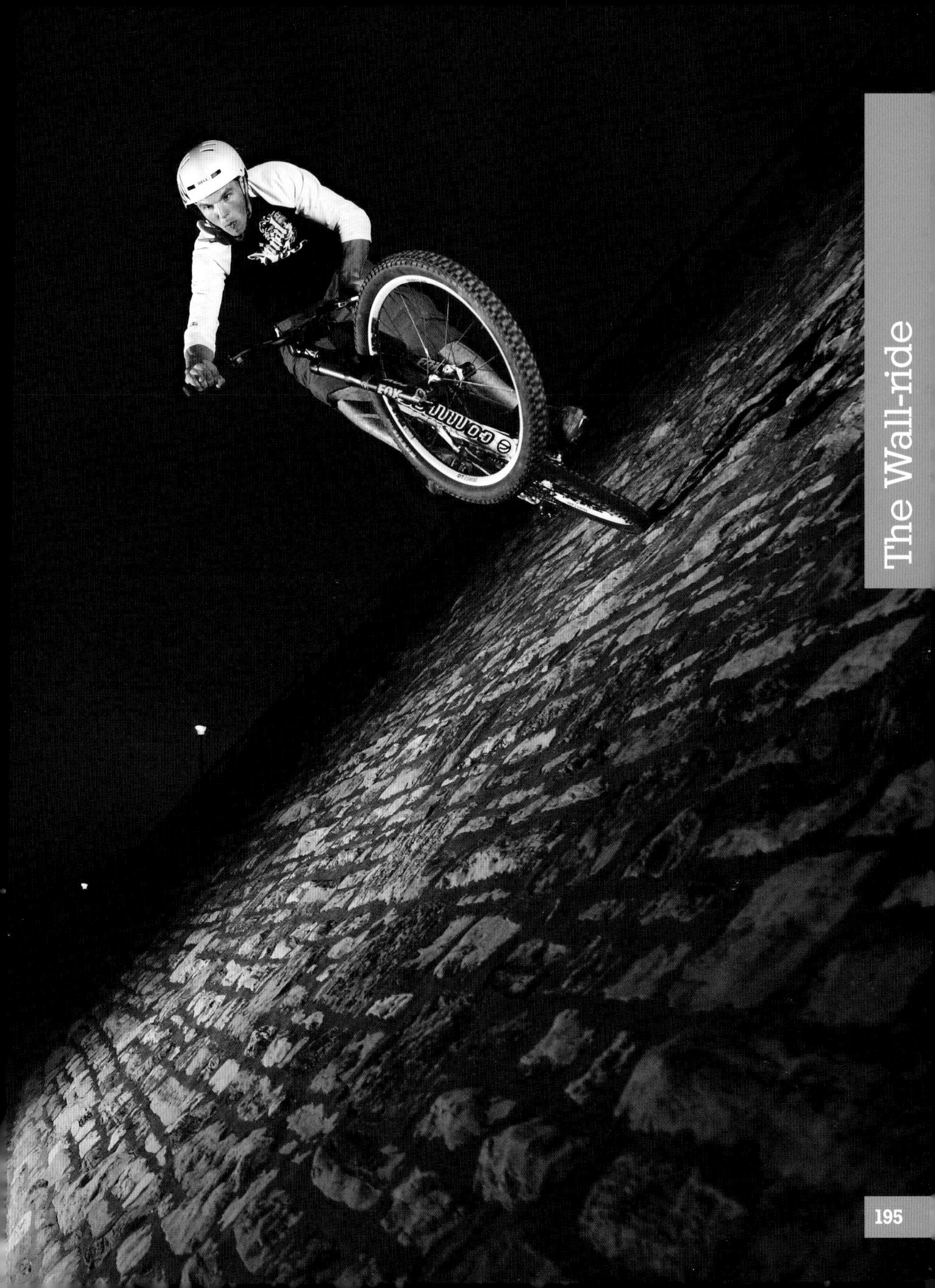
FOX

Go online and visit www.mtbtricks.co.uk for videos and tutorials

# " THE WALL-RIDE IS AS SIMPLE AS RIDING AROUND A CORNER! "

**Every time I've sat down to write about a trick for this book I start by thinking what I like about it, I usually come to the conclusion that it (no matter which one) is my favourite move. The wall-ride actually must be very close to my favourite move though. It's such a dynamique piece of riding, it oozes quality. Riders who can use wall-rides; enjoy wall-rides even, are often very proficient all-round riders. That fits too; because the wall-ride is a very diverse move that will actually work for you in many different places, opening up new lines to your riding spots that before were for Spiderman alone. We need to be clear that a number of elements need to be in place before you can wall-ride. Actually it's a bit like a free-ride drop in the sense that; the real skill is realising when those elements are present and taking the opportunity.**

Over the years I've seen riders take these elements and twist the rules to make a wall-ride work in the most ridiculous places. I've tried a few in my time and I remember the day I spotted a wall-ride that would take some serious crashing before I could string all the elements together and make it.......

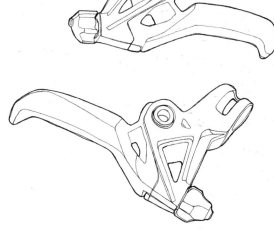

The way to look at wall-rides and make sense of them is to imagine them as a corner. That is effectively what you do to make them work. The 'trick' is gaining enough momentum and angle from an entry point that you can stick to the wall long enough to ride across to your exit point. The wall-ride is as simple as riding around a corner!

That is exactly where you should begin learning too. A simple berm at a BMX track or 4X course is perfect. Even a quarter-pipe ramps can work for this practice, so your local skate-park is sure to have an obstacle that can work.

# " IT'S THE COMPRESSION AND MOMENTUM THAT WILL KEEP YOU STUCK TO THE WALL "

Ride at the obstacle with good momentum and just feel the sensation of compression as you turn the bike sharply in the peak of the turn, also notice how your body angle is leant in to the apex of the turn. Once you have noticed this try to exaggerate it – imagine a mirror on a ceiling directly above you in the turn, try and get as flat an image of you in that mirror. This gets you used to the horizontal position needed to wall-ride. 'Railing' the turn has taught us the now obvious elements needed to wall-ride: entry, wall and exit. The task at hand is to start looking for a suitable place to try it out. This is the exciting bit because your imagination will run riot at this point. I find myself going as far as looking at buildings and thinking "If I was 30ft tall I could hit that car park entry ramp, jump

to a wall-ride on the side of the town hall, and then land in the slope of that awning outside the butchers shop." I'm not being mad though - this is how you learn – especially once you spot a suitable wall that works for your actual height and not my imaginary 30-foot self, then it will all pay off.

If you are struggling to find a good wall to practise then try making one with a simple kicker ramp like the one pictured and start using a grass bank as the wall. Hitting the kicker as your entry and using the small amount of air-time to move into the position required to compress and turn the bike off the wall. Remember that it's the compression and momentum that will keep you stuck to the wall long enough to rail the turn and hop back off into your exit point.

**Speed = compression in the turn – giving you gravity defying skills**

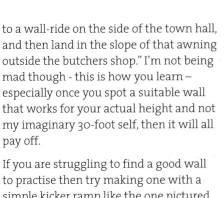

"When someone told me I had a million views on YouTube I couldn't believe it - that was in just one week. It's amazing what has happened to me through releasing 'that video'... I was just doing what I do and never expected this kind of reaction."

**Danny MacAskill**
YouTube sensation and
Street Trials genius

# DREAM TRICKS

In this last section I want to set you off on the trail of the really big moves – 360 spin and back-flip. You will probably have heard of these moves and seen them on internet and TV – I've been riding bike shows for years and we use both mentioned moves as finale tricks. These exciting moves are very difficult but still achievable for a rider who wants them enough – practising them in the correct environment will be a key factor.

# PROGRESSION

**You could be drawn into thinking these closing chapters signal some kind of 'cap' to what you can learn on a bike – that this is the very best stuff that I saved for the end. Well I do love these moves and they certainly belong at the end of this book but in no-way do they even touch on what is possible on a bicycle these days – if you are serious about riding bikes then these advanced moves mark the beginning of your hopes rather then any kind of ending. The progression of modern riding is simply ridiculous and it's moving forward every single day. You can keep up-to-date with that progression via some websites that I will point you to later.**

Hopefully in these pages you have found inspiration and enjoyment – through a triangle of words, pictures and web content. The 360 and Back-flip will lead you down a path that doesn't come with instructions because the whole development process of action sports are driven by individuals expressing themselves through their sport. In modern riding, tricks like 1080s (3 full spins) back-flip Tailwhips (flip with a frame whip of the bike combined), front-flips, double back-flips and flairs (back-flip 180) have all been done, and some of them very regularly. Those mentioned are big moves, the big banger of the firework display. Some riders prefer to be far more technical with their riding and instead of the 'big banger' they focus on technicality that will be appreciated by their peers – a great

example of this would be the brakeless BMX movement where riders pull amazing moves on their bikes but as you would guess – without brakes.

The point I'd like to make is don't let my words and choices dictate yours. I sincerely hope this book has led you to trying something new on your bike but should also have awakened thoughts about what you do well, what suits your style etc. Similarly you will have found areas that didn't really 'float your boat' so to speak; that's all part of your progression so listen to those feelings. Keeping the focus on fun will be what leads you to great skills. If you're enjoying yourself then repetition will be easier and the learning curve steep.

> **KEEPING THE FOCUS ON FUN WILL BE WHAT LEADS YOU TO GREAT SKILLS**

# BEGIN TO SPIN: THE 360

There aren't many moves more impressive than the 360. This exciting jump manoeuvre will take plenty of practice and probably some crashing, but I will point you in the right direction for safe learning and padding. Turning a complete turn whilst in the air is never going to be completely safe but don't let that put you off – you're pushing the limits now so no point in self doubt.

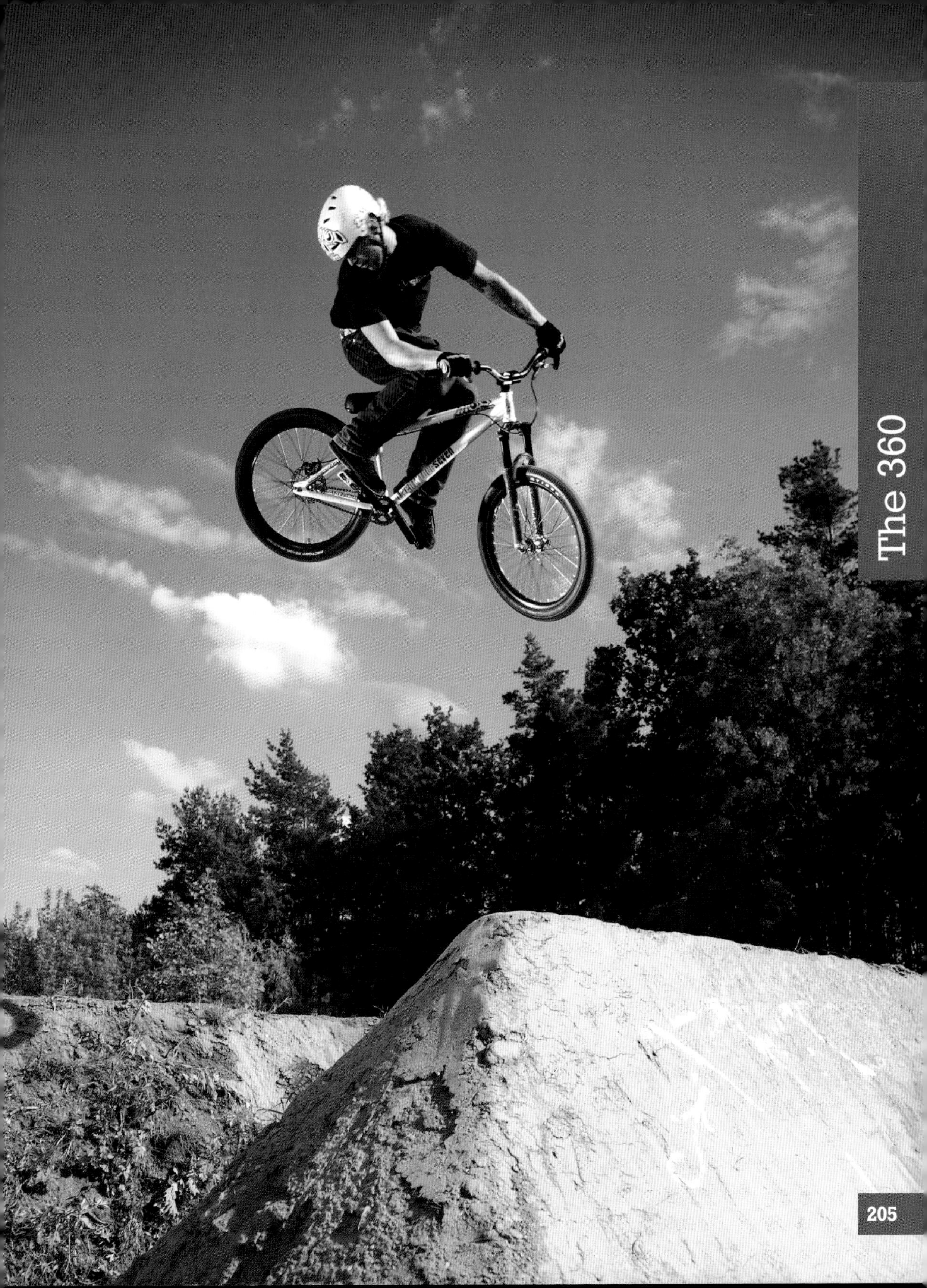

## " I'M SURE BY NOW YOU'VE DISCOVERED THAT EVERY MOVE WILL TAKE DETERMINATION "

When performing in bike shows as a pro rider, I always enjoy the reaction when the 360 is unleashed, it's always a very popular moment in the show. Some of the talented riders I work with add in other tricks whilst 360-ing to make it look even more crazy! I've always been a fan of the simple 360 however. When it's done big, bold and really simple this move has so much grace that it would be really hard to top. That grace comes from the body movement needed to control the rotation. If you spin too quickly then the over-rotation will lead to disaster, too slow and you'll get the obvious opposite result. The top boys will put 360s into places on trail and jumps that I find unbelievable. It's one thing to learn the move on your favourite ramp, quite another to bust it out off a 30ft drop that you only saw 20-minutes earlier?

Go online and visit www.mtbtricks.co.uk for videos and tutorials

That scenario sounds ridiculous but back in 2006 I was watching the footage from the now famous Crankworz event in Canada. Top freeride pro Darren Berrecloth was in his run and approaching a huge 30ft descent of a ladder, down into a right-handed burmed corner that would propel him down into the finishing arena and the final jumps. As 'Bearclaw' (as he's known) approached the drop, no one could have imagined the move he'd decided on. Darren is very proficient at 360s and that was proved as he gracefully spun the bike left off the edge of the abyss. Turning slowly but in full control Darren 360ed down and landed smoothly, immediately railing the right handed burm. He shot down towards the finish area with the crowd going insane.

Bearclaw's antics are a great example of the extreme use of a 360; difficult obstacle, big drop and landing into an opposite corner! It just doesn't get gnarlier than that.

The simple 3 is always a treat though and I've always loved seeing riders like Grant 'Chopper' Fielder, Sam Pilgrim or Chris Smith pull huge versions in competition events. These guys make it look unbelievably easy... I wish I could say it was easy but I'm sure by now you've discovered that every move will take determination.

The 360

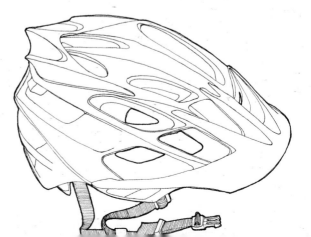

So the first thing to decide when choosing this move is where you're going to try it. Your local jumps are obvious because the take-off will be familiar and the atmosphere comforting but let me put a small downer on it - which I do with regret because I don't like to be negative – but this is for a positive result. I think of new tricks or moves as physical objects that once learned I own. I imagine showing friends and family the finished product, pictures and video of how I use it. A boy with a new toy basically: "look at me doing this 360 here Dad", "this is me and the 360 in Los Angeles Mum." You get the general idea. So with that basis in mind think how important 'owning' this trick will be to you? Now if I put a price on it – say if you gave me £70 in return for being able to do it instantly – you'd almost certainly pay the price wouldn't you. It really is that easy though. Instead of taking a gamble on it at the local jump, take a car trip to the nearest foam pit (see next section about great places to ride and chat) and try it in complete safety. The foam will allow you to try the system I lay out here as many times as you like, completely safe. After a good session in the foam you'll take the knowledge back to your normal jump and apply the technique with confidence and determination. The move will be in your bag, mistakes will have been made safely and you can start showing everybody your new best toy.

The simple way for me to describe what you need to do is think about the mantra I'm giving you: head, shoulders, hips and keep looking. As you go up the ramp for take off start in the direction you wish to spin – your comfortable way to spin will most likely be away from your front foot – now imagine you did nothing else other than this. You would just jump off at an angle because at speed there is only

so much turn you'll fit in on the take-off. Instead think about turning but continue to twist your body. Lots of first time 360-ers will throw their back into the move but try to concentrate on putting your chin on your shoulder, as it hits continue the twist with chin on shoulder and let shoulders spin through movement in your waist, that will then bring movement in your hips. Think about those three elements of your movement, and when all three have gone through that motion keep looking for the landing – it won't be as far away as you think. If you spin out of the ramp and look hard for the landing ramp, chances are you'll find it.

Safety is the key; determination will come from confident beginnings in learning and success will follow. Now watch the podcast and get that move drummed in, think hard about the mantra and what the action is doing. Don't be shy to bore every one once it's in the bag!

"

*IF YOU SPIN OUT OF THE RAMP AND LOOK HARD FOR THE LANDING RAMP, CHANCES ARE YOU'LL FIND IT*

"

The 360

**Head to chin, twist those shoulders and follow with the hips**

# THE BACK FLIP

**I**f you're anything like me then you'll be reading this bit of the book long before you should – I'm always skipping through details on video games to see how to do the bits my son and I want to try. This isn't a video game so by all means read through etc but please don't start attempting back-flips before you're ready. That sounds crazy doesn't it: "try a back-flip?" Don't be struck by a defeatist attitude though, this stuff is possible and as long as we keep the attempts in a safe place the chances of success is good.

**Trials' riding doesn't have much call for back-flips, so it was never high on my agenda of techniques to learn. I'd always watched my favourite BMX riders do them and think how cool it would be to do one. It didn't feel possible though and I spent 10 years as a pro not considering them in any way.**

It was at a skate-park with my friends when the first experience with them set me on a path that would effectively change my career, my riding and my life. I had been bombing around this park for a couple of hours, and as always usual for me in a skate park I'd run out of ideas and energy; I was ready to leave. The friends I was with still had some steam and I waited for them to finish, sitting on my bike at the top of a big roll-in ramp facing the foam-pit (see next chapter on what that is). I'd never really bothered with foam-pits, I had no need but for some reason I thought I'd spend the last bit of my ride doing some silly tricks into the foam. My first ride in was not good and I landed really steep; and that bad jump got me thinking about how a back-flip could work – so I gave it a go. The first attempt was actually not too bad - I thought I'd fix it with more speed. The second go didn't go well at all, I seemed to stall upside down and I landed on my head. Instead of taking a considered moment to realise more speed hadn't helped I decided to go really fast. The result was a complete disaster; resulting in a landing from a height that not even a foam pit could help with – I broke my back in five places and was looking at the end of my riding career!

After that day I inevitably laid down for quite a while...very restful. I played video games and was happy that everything was healing, my legs still worked and it could have been worse I guess. Physically I was on the mend, mentally I couldn't believe I'd

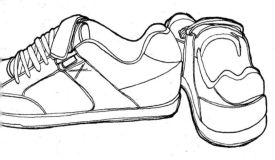

made such a bad job of it and knew I was always going to watch other riders pull the back-flips, I'd never again be able to say "it must be cool to do that trick" all I'd ever be able to say was "I will never do that trick". My imagination had been taken away! Screw that – I spent the next few months watching every video of flips I could find. I had to nail that trick or I'd never be the same rider again.

Once back on my feet I had to change the way I trained to accommodate the weakness in my back. I turned it into the strongest part of me. I then had to address the mental damage and that could only be fixed by learning to back flip. That is another story altogether but the pictures in this book should give you an idea of the result – fixed bloody-minded determination is a powerful thing.

"

# FIXED BLOODY-MINDED DETERMINATION IS A POWERFUL THING

"

Go online and visit www.mtbtricks.co.uk for videos and tutorials

The backlip

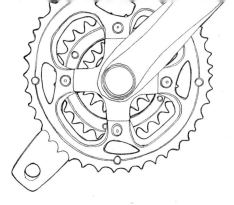

My story could be the example of why you shouldn't learn back-flips, however I'd argue it's nothing more than an example of what happens when you make rash decisions. Once I was fixed and serious about learning I found safe places to learn it, the original foam pit I used was famous for being very dangerous and it no longer exists. If you go to a proper riding centre like the ones in the following chapter the result will be a far more enjoyable day, with far more success. Use my story to push you forward not hold you back. Let's get down to the nitty-gritty of how and then it's really up to you if you should.

If I told you to 'ghost' your bike out of a ramp you would be very excited to see how it naturally did a back-flip all by itself. The transition of the take-off will naturally loop the bike. The secret to pulling a flip is to go with the transition and commit to sitting in to your bike and like the 360 – look for the landing – you'll find it's somewhere over your head.

So approach the ramp into the foam pit with good speed (fast enough that if you didn't flip you'd travel half the length

## THE SECRET TO PULLING A FLIP IS TO GO WITH THE TRANSITION AND COMMIT

of the pit). As you come up the take off commit yourself towards a sitting position, holding yourself in a strong position and look over your head. Your bum and momentum will swing you under the bike and the idea is your spin created through holding that look for the landing will keep the spin going. As you spot your landing it will feel natural to relax slightly and start to prepare for the landing. This point of recognition for the landing will be very hard to spot at first; stay relaxed though and let plenty of attempts sort that out. You need to become familiar with the sensation and soon you'll be pin-pointing that landing every time.

Leave the pit: I don't want to encourage you any further than this point. If you have 'got the bug' from my text and have used the video to get yourself attempting the trick into a foam-pit then the next step must be your decision. The natural progression would be from foam to a resi-ramp; a jump with a sprung landing that works as a pretty safe place to try a flip for real. You can do it if you want it enough.

*Commit your head into the flip – look for that landing over your head*

# GREAT PLACES TO RIDE AND CHAT

Throughout I've been talking about foam-pits, skate parks and places you should go for great advice and support. In this chapter I will talk you through some of my favourite spots. I will also point you towards the websites that will help you explore all there is to find in the world of cycling. The internet has had a huge impact on sport, books like this wouldn't be possible for an example. I've not had to get bogged down with technical analysis of the moves as you've progressed, simply because your understanding has advanced and the video clips should be showing you all you need to know. Beyond this format, the internet has put us all in touch with immediate information. There are huge but diverse communities available on the web that have exactly what you're looking for.

The places to ride will come down to what you want to learn. Many riding parks exist these days. Again the online communities are the place to find out about riding venues but below are a couple that I really enjoy. The skate parks are of great interest in my opinion. These facilities are so powerful in the learning process that they shouldn't be ignored. It's a great day out if nothing else. So check out my suggestions, but again look to online friends to find the right one for you. The travelling might seem tricky but just think what you could gain from a few hours in the car.

# MY FAVOURITE MOUNTAIN BIKE RIDING CENTRES

Specialist mountain biking centres are popping up all over the country at the moment. Most venues feature a central café and car park with marked riding-routes heading away in varying technical difficulties or length; eventually bringing you back to the centre. These parks are one of the most enjoyable ways to ride MTB these days; the riding terrain is usually of an amazing standard; including rocky descents, tough climbs and even North Shore. What's North Shore I hear you ask?

North Shore riding originated in Canada and was used to build ride-ways through dense forests and then caught on as a riding genre all of its own. The courses consist of wooden ladders and drops, see-saws and wooden burmed corners – basically anything goes. These days you'll find a bit of North Shore in most cross-country trail centres, usually as part of the cross country course. The 'skinny' is a very popular obstacle that is basically riding something very narrow. That curb practice will become very useful on these.

### Afan:

Afan Argoed is also in South Wales and is perhaps more trail orientated than the downhill focused Cwm Carn. The many routes at Afan will keep you interested and offer quite a few lengths of ride – you can also jump from one route to another whilst out riding as they criss-cross at a few points. The café is awesome – basically take that for granted. I have ridden most of the trails here and enjoy them all, you could spend a few days here getting a different ride each time – so if a mountain bike weekend is on the cards then check out accommodation near Afan. There's great surfing just down the road in Porthcawl as well.

### Cwm Carn:

Cwm carn is one of the leading centres with an up-lift ferry service for the downhill riders and an outstanding cross-country trail that includes a free-ride route at the top of the course. A great centre full of friendly faces and like most centres these days – the Café does great food. I love the downhill course here but mostly ride the XC trail, it's a good forty minute ride that has everything I need to make me feel I've been 'mountain bike riding' so that's about perfect really.

## THESE PARKS ARE ONE OF THE MOST ENJOYABLE WAYS TO RIDE MTB

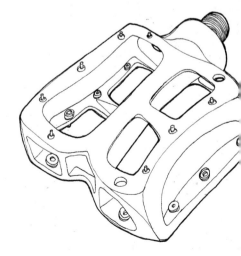

# SKATE PARKS

Originally these parks were, as the name suggests, for skating but in the late seventies BMX riders began a scene that would see bikes in these parks. These days it is very common to see a skate park filled with riders on skate boards, roller blades, MTBs and even micro scooters. There really aren't any rules on 'what' any more so don't feel your bike doesn't belong. The real key to having an enjoyable day at a skate park is to go with as many pads as you can and always wear a helmet.

You may find the environment quite intimidating at first, everyone will look like they know what they are doing. Rest assured that they are all very nice people and the best thing to do if you are unsure is to ask. Remember that everyone had to start somewhere.

### Adrenaline Alley (Corby):
This park is an absolute dream. Every possible obstacle is there including all the safety ramps like foam-pits and resi-ramps. I've ridden this one a lot and it is full of friendly faces. A day trip to this place will see your riding ability soar and the same for your confidence. Look out for some crazy action from top pro riders in here as well. The moves on show by these guys are just ridiculous and will make you desperate to learn new moves and progress. Corby has a great foam pit as well so if you want to use this feature in your practice then Adrenalin Alley could be the perfect visit for you.

**Unit 23 (Dumbarton):**
Is another spot that will improve your riding but it's harder to find than Adrenaline alley. There are three massive rooms of ramps, including one room devoted entirely to resi-ramps and a foam-pit. I spent the whole day in that room once, just so much fun. This park has also got considerable 'pro' traffic so don't be surprised if some big name riders walk in and lay down some huge moves. The staff are super friendly and will be very keen for you to enjoy yourself.

> **THESE DAYS IT IS VERY COMMON TO SEE A SKATE PARK FILLED WITH RIDERS ON SKATE BOARDS, ROLLER BLADES, MTBS AND EVEN MICRO SCOOTERS**

# THE COMMUNITY

As someone who rides around on a bike you are part of a huge and very diverse community. There really is no reason to ever have a question about riding (where, when or how) unanswered these days. Monthly magazines like Mountain Biking UK are full of features and product reviews that will keep you informed. This magazine is also a great monthly point of inspiration. Even I find the will to ride subside sometimes but just flicking through this magazine and looking at great riders doing great things makes me want to ride.

## Online community:

www.bikeradar.com with millions of visitors each month 'Radar' is by far the most popular cycling website in the UK. There are categories for MTB and all it's disciplines such as Dirt-Jump, Cross Country and Downhill. If there's any questions or interest that has grown from reading this book then get over to BikeRadar where you'll find like-minded people only too willing to help and inspire further.

This site is also the inspiration for an awesome annual event called 'BikeRadar Live'. The event is designed for everyone and captures the spirit of cycling. The World's top riders turn up and ride alongside people who are brand new to the sport - it's fantastic!

## Have fun:

The bike is often portrayed as a useful form of transport that can help us battle global warming, or a weapon of torture that we should use to whip our bodies back into shape from the excesses of modern life. What I hope this book has done over all the things it can teach you is to look at your bike, and how you use it. Bikes are great fun and the words, pictures and video will hopefully have inspired you to try some new things that will see your confidence sore and your enjoyment of bikes increase beyond recognition.

So I wish you happy riding and look forward to seeing you out on the trail, skate park or jump spot. One thing is for sure I will continue to enjoy riding bikes in as many different ways as I can, and if you have been inspired to do similar then I'm a very happy bike rider indeed.

**Martyn Ashton**

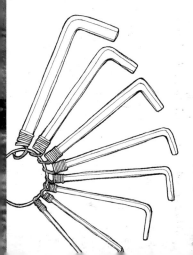

# THANKS & DEDICATION

Writing a book isn't easy - **Jane Robinson** took this idea seriously and helped me realise a life-long dream. Thank you Jane.

Whilst I have this chance there are things I must say and more people to thank.

**Lisa:** all my gratitude, love and admiration are yours.
I'm so proud of the family we've become. The letter-box and a Raleigh Burner seem a long time ago now - but my life has had meaning ever since that moment. I love you.

Whilst shooting this book I had a truly great time, lots of laughs and a couple of sopping-wet cold days that made me want to cry - but it was predominantly laughs.

On this journey I stood alongside a truly great artist, visionary and friend - **Robin Kitchin**. In my line of work I meet many extraordinary people, none have ever impressed and influenced me more than Robin. Cheers dude, you're a legend.

**Dad**: for the power to dream. Give 100% to achieve your dreams. Your belief allows me to believe anything is possible. 'Que Sera, Sera'

**Mum:** for Love. All our growing families are in joyful orbit around you, stable through the gravity of your heart.

**Alfie:** for Joy. Every smile makes my heart fly man. Your energy will ruin my knees!

My brothers **Lee & Andy:** for determination. I constantly try to keep up with your examples and it isn't easy.

This book is dedicated to my **Nan 'Eton-Wick'**. How so much strength can come from so small a person I will never know.